Epistemic Ruptures, Insurgent Philosophy

CANNAE
PRESS

Epistemic Ruptures|2

Epistemic Ruptures, Insurgent Philosophy

A. Shahid Stover

Were it not for the cold, how would the heat of Thy words prevail, O expounder of the worlds?[1]

-Baha'u'llah (1817-1892)

---

[1] Baha'u'llah, *Writings of Baha'u'llah: A Compilation*, (New Delhi: Bahai Publishing Trust, 2006) p.962.

Dedicated to my Grandmother Eva,
in Loving Memory.

To Nardiye and Tadeos, with Love, always.

Much respect to *The Brotherwise Dispatch* editorial cipher – Sultan Stover, Dario Sanchez-Kennedy and Robert J. Jackson.

Much gratitude to LaRose T. Parris for her ongoing intellectual camaraderie that includes close, careful and critical readings of this work.

A. Shahid Stover

Epistemic Ruptures, Insurgent Philosophy

CANNAE PRESS

New York

Epistemic Ruptures, Insurgent Philosophy
Copyright © 2022 by Artemus Stover

All rights reserved. No part of this book may be reproduced or transmitted in any form or by any means without written permission from the author.

0 5 2 3 1 8 4 4 2

Published by
Cannae Press
P.O. Box 460
New York, NY 10276
cannaepress.com

Cover Design and Illustration by VC Design Studios
vcdesignstudios.com

Library of Congress Control Number: 2022915228
ISBN: 978-1-7335510-3-8 (paperback)
ISBN: 978-1-7335510-4-5 (ebook)

****

Contents

Preface 29

Epistemic Ruptures

insurgent philosophy and the Real 35

emancipatory relevance of intellectual rigor 38

insurgent philosophy in the Raw 46

academics, typical readers & insurgent philosophy ... 57

Critical Encounters

'being-in-the-world' and Coates 65

oppositional thought after the fall 81

Reveries of the Ronin

green tea, cigars & existential liberation 89

café culture, intellectual engagement & the Ronin 92

allegory of the Ronin 101

Emancipatory Epilogue

global pandemic, Black liberation & the plague of Empire 107

Working Concepts, Discursive Terms & Unfixed Definitions 127

Preface

What happens when philosophy refuses to limit the horizon of emancipatory thought to the academic systematization of specialized knowledge? Aside from demanding severe levels of concentration from readers, the pathways such insurgent thought takes, rarely cedes its discursive trajectory prior to the action of thinking itself. Black liberation discourse in particular, in wrestling with the exceptional antagonism of ascendant humanity disclosed through lived Black experience within the context of a western imperialist continuum, allows for a tremendous epistemic upheaval of imagination, concepts, notions and ideas against established structures of meaning.

As such, my writing leaves in its wake the safe harbor of acceptable epistemic preoccupations, and ventures forth towards the perilous deep of intellectual engagement, situated adrift disastrous waves of history that actively mediate against the manifest intentionality of my work as a philosopher, an unsanctioned thinker, an outsider, a radical autonomous intellectual, a Ronin.

And yet, although to be a Ronin is indicative of a particular penchant for radical autonomous intellectual endeavor; to understand what is meant by conceptualizing the Ronin as a particular mode of intellectual engagement, as a lived rhythm of praxis and way of 'being-in-the-world', is not just meant a thinker who thrives outside of the institutional confines of the

Academy. Rather, the Ronin is an allegorical designation of singular commitment to intellectual endeavor that manifests a zealous disregard for the need to pursue well-trodden and socially celebrated paths of Academic prestige and/or mainstream literary success. This is not to disparage either of these choices, except insofar as each might pretend to assume a monopoly on legitimating the scope of intellectual endeavor itself.

Indeed, by eschewing the cult of unbridled pursuit of profit over people and celebrity over principle, even in the face of financial hardship and socio-cultural isolation, to be a Ronin is to creatively flourish by the very choice to resist temptations of irresponsibility that lead towards a fatal epistemic embrace of the marketable, the familiar, and the popular.

Essentially, the writings that comprise *Epistemic Ruptures, Insurgent Philosophy* were initially published in *The Brotherwise Dispatch*, with the exception of "Oppositional Thought After the Fall", which was published in *Connections*, a peer-reviewed e-journal of the European Network in Universal and Global History in the field of transnational, transregional and world histories based in Leipzig, Germany.

As such, in spite of the growing global relevance of my work, or maybe precisely because of it, with *Epistemic Ruptures, Insurgent Philosophy*, I felt it necessary to convey just how much, in my own case, the intellectual trajectory that comes with being a Ronin, simultaneously involves initiating both a rebirth of philosophy in the world outside the academic establishment, as well as a return to the café as a contested site of intellectual endeavor and creative undertaking accessible to everyday people. And it is by reveling in such a spirit of autonomy that *Epistemic Ruptures, Insurgent Philosophy* unites essays, ruptures and reviews that communicate a dynamic depth of literary tension and radical intellectual activity situated against predominant imperialist ideological currents of advanced neo-liberal capitalist globalization that permeate a bourgeoning afterlife of post-millennium café culture in New York City.

And yet, since the onset of a global pandemic that shows no signs of abating, the question need not be limited to musing on about the continued social relevance of the café in relation to grassroots literary culture at the margins of institutional sanction, for even the very existence of café culture itself is being fundamentally called into question, if not at least seriously teetering on the brink of insignificance.

To be clear, not all writers are suited to sustaining such a concentrated focus on their intellectual endeavors amidst a lively, unruly, and yes at times inhospitable atmosphere experienced by constantly frequenting a vast archipelago of New York City cafés.

Indeed, writing in cafés amongst everyday people who don't particularly give a damn about insurgent philosophy, existential liberation critique or Black radical discourse, is an exuberantly consistent reminder that the world inhabited by independent intellectuals outside of the academic establishment offers no guarantees, no welcome, no acclaim and certainly no damn pension.

What a lived marginality to the imperial mainstream does have to offer however, in contrast to the menacing neo-liberal lethargy of thought currently afflicting the Academy itself, is the possibility of a critically robust vitality of intellectual endeavor that refuses to barter away the emancipatory relevance of intellectual rigor to gain a wider receptivity.

For when writing drives your lived rhythm of praxis and hence constitutes your presence towards self, intersubjective resonance towards one another and engagement in the world as a philosopher and radical autonomous intellectual, your literary intentionality and your work rise to prominence as the horizon of action itself. As such, who has the time to write profitable, yet disposable works that pander to a lowest common denominator of thinking?

Epistemic Ruptures

insurgent philosophy and the Real – Philosophy is often reduced to a mere discipline amongst other academic disciplines, a neatly polished rhetorical exercise towards continually revisiting the systematic certainty of completely developed *fixed* formulae through a discursive showcase of redundant facts, ready-made questions and the sedentary logic of positivism. However, the analytical quest for clarity of thought through pedestrian language betrays a false nobility that veils the very objectivity it lauds with a fetish of myth posturing as rhetorical transparency within which reside the seeds of epistemic closure as performative harmony with the Real.

Insurgent philosophy moves discursively from its genesis in the Raw of coloniality towards interrogations of the Real that confront the *normative gaze* of western imperialist power by resisting the *biopolitical pacification* of human 'being'. For the Real constantly acquaints human 'being' with the possibility of abdicating human *subjectivity* in exchange for an epistemologically sanctioned 'objecthood' of *identity* characterized as a substantive *empirical self-as-rational animality*. However, insurgent philosophical endeavor calls into question the nature of this ossification of situated consciousness into 'objecthood', and aids in enunciating Revolt towards inciting openings of human 'being' as *lived rhythm of praxis* towards human subjectivity necessitated through a decision of spiritual upheaval against the menacing gravity of *overdetermination-from-without* by established power.

Insurgent philosophy thus constitutes an emancipatory ontological wager of human 'being' originating as a discursive response to the disaster of coloniality in the Raw that situates the singularity of lived Black experience as an *exceptional antagonism* within modernity as imposed by western imperialist power. As such, philosophy at an insurgent register interrogates the Real and enunciates Revolt against Empire with critical conceptual interpretations that exert a discursive emancipatory pressure upon the normative gaze towards potentialities of introducing epistemological ruptures; thus breaching a coercive anonymity of biopolitical pacification against human 'being' that inscribes modernity with a structural-inert violence that weighs upon Black subjectivity with an intense socio-ontological severity and unprecedented geohistorical imperative towards the universal.

No doubt, for thought to assert an objective philosophical posture in relation to the hegemony of Empire, not only endorses socio-ontological retreat from confronting the Raw of coloniality that situates valid attempts at epistemological opposition within a dogmatic regurgitation of established structures of meaning and a sanctioned renewal of conventional wisdom, but ultimately revalidates a replication of discursive fidelity to the normative gaze of western imperialist power.

Insurgent philosophical endeavor draws its epistemological sustenance from the Raw, an intense proximity of lived experience that unchains emancipatory potentialities of thought from discursive fidelity to the

Real of western imperialist power as obscured under the dim lights of epistemic closure through logical positivist analysis and poststructuralist sophistry.

Oppositional philosophy, regardless of whether in concert with continental or analytical traditions, by deriving fundamental epistemological precepts and core teleological conclusions from modernity itself, ultimately reproduces a western imperialist continuum even while challenging its contemporary guise of advanced neo-liberal capitalist globalization with state socialist or communist variants.

Whereas *insurgent philosophy*, by choosing to begin in the intensity of disaster as racist dehumanization and coloniality in the Raw that structurally positions an imperial mainstream-as-civil society at the lived expense of a socio-ontological underground of modernity in its wake, confronts Empire with an emancipatory universality towards constitutive potentialities of human 'being' and human liberation which undermine a western imperialist continuum by destabilizing the epistemic conditions of its possibility.

emancipatory relevance of intellectual rigor – Readers often measure their initial approach to philosophy with overinflated valuations that rest upon the cozy comforts of common sense, overreliance on the dogmatic religion of routine thought, overindulgence in the security of familiar words, and overemphasis on the tranquility of everyday consensus. However, it is precisely such prescriptive means of epistemological harmony with the normative gaze of Empire that philosophy actively labors against.

Indeed, Empire *overdetermines-from-without*, imposing *biopolitical pacification* upon human 'being' towards reducing entire populations from lived potentialities of human subjectivity to the materialist determinism of an 'empirical self' that effortlessly acclimates to established power as dominated non-resisting masses and bewildered herds of rational animality. Objective violence and miseducation of soul work in tandem to constitute the normative gaze of Empire with monotonous systematic efficiency towards ensuring that the *underground of modernity*, who suffer perpetually through a lived fatigue of racist dehumanization and coloniality, do not often choose to embrace emancipatory imperatives of responsibility for human liberation at every crossroads of historical possibility. The normative gaze thus aims at preventing uprisings like Ferguson and Baltimore from becoming even more frequent phenomena by encouraging everyday people to actively participate in our own biopolitical pacification, even as structural-inert conditions of oppression and exploitation mercilessly engulf our 'being-in-the-world'.

Under such conditions, when the masses are clearly not in open rebellion against Empire, does not the very enunciation of Revolt realize itself as an avant-garde trajectory of thought that ultimately risks exacerbating existing epistemological tensions between intellectual rigor, emancipatory relevance and popular accessibility? Without question, efforts towards reducing the scope of emancipatory relevance to a mere therapeutic narrative of pragmatic assimilation into the imperial mainstream-as-civil society leave the radical imagination stranded in a logical positivist temperament of popular abdication to the normative gaze. For the normative gaze imposes a coercive anonymity upon human agency by violently inscribing fixed boundaries upon the horizon of lived Black experience – boundaries that necessarily mediate against insurgent potentialities of thought by positing the Real of a western imperialist continuum as the historical culmination of all that is existentially possible.

Insurgent philosophy thus pierces the normative gaze, disrupting the topography of imperial coherence and unarticulated structures of meaning that preempt both the enunciation of cognition, perception and imagination in ordinary discourse, and the systematic organization of formal logic in the Academy. As such, if insurgent philosophy does not first provoke the reader to transcend the comforting rationality of discursive familiarity, by what measure can such thought claim to be challenging the normative gaze of established power? Indeed, how often does the socio-historical relevance of emancipatory praxis outpace the discursive capacity of the imperial mainstream-as-civil society? And, how might well intentioned oppositional strategies meant to frame Black liberation discourse within the stable rationality of popular accessibility, necessarily facilitate an epistemic subjugation of insurgent thought by the normative gaze of western imperialist power?

"Give us the facts, we will take care of the philosophy."[2] Only several years removed from liberating himself from human bondage, that's the exact advice Douglass received from some of his fellow abolitionists, precisely as he began embarking on what would become a lifelong trajectory of intellectual engagement against western imperialist power as it was then constituted through direct human slavery. Although such pragmatic suggestions ultimately served as encouragement towards his Promethean autobiographical endeavors, Douglass clearly understood that facts in and of themselves, even facts regarding the indisputable horror of first-hand accounts about the violent regulatory imposition of slavery upon human 'being', are too often subsumed within established structures of meaning. Thereby neutralizing potentialities of insurrection against human slavery by epistemologically reinforcing the sovereign legitimacy of the socio-historical conditions of its possibility.

---

[2] Frederick Douglass, *Life and Times of Frederick Douglass*, (New York: Collier Books, 1892, 1962) p.217.

Consequently, Douglass never truly heeded such well-intentioned counsel by his close allies in the anti-slavery movement. No longer satisfied with the vitally important task of giving empirical account of oppression, Douglass chose to openly think against oppression, as the insurgent intellectual prowess that pervades all three of his autobiographies and five massive volumes of essays and lectures unequivocally discloses. "I could not always follow the injunction, for I was now reading and writing. New views on the subject were being presented to my mind. It did not entirely satisfy me to *narrate* wrongs – I felt like *denouncing* them."[3] In this Douglass remained discursively undaunted, even as his abolitionist comrades began noticing that proclaiming him as a "fugitive slave lecturer"[4] became less and less believable to burgeoning crowds gathered to hear him speak out against human slavery from the vantage point of having actually freed himself from such brutal materialist ontological tyranny of social death.

Indeed, the more Douglass triumphed at interpreting the meaning and insurgency of his own existence, rather than merely statically regurgitating the dehumanizing visceral facts that situate and implicate lived Black experience – "People doubted if I had ever been a slave. They said I did not talk like a slave, look like a slave, or act like a slave, and that they believed I had never been south of the Mason

---

[3] Douglass, *Life and Times*, p.217. emphasis in original.
[4] Douglass, ibid.

and Dixon's line."[5] No doubt, for how could anyone expecting an example of racially dehumanized 'objecthood' and walking social death seeking pity and beseeching approbation, truly be prepared for the towering unapologetic human figure of Douglass enunciating potentialities of human solidarity in Revolt against tyranny by manifesting the rebirth of *human subjectivity-as-lived universal* through emancipatory praxis against the ontological weight of social death perpetuated by *chattel* slavery? It seems that even expressed sympathy for the legal abolition of human slavery within the confines of a nation-state, does little to alleviate an unreflective culturally inbred weight of racist skepticism towards the possibility of human *subjectivity* outside the anthropological coordinates of 'white' *identity* as embodiment of the universal.

Thus, Black intellectual engagement has an intense social burden and ontological severity associated with it, precisely because of the exceptional antagonism which exists between the assertion of Black subjectivity-as-human 'being' and the imposition of modernity onto the world by a western imperialist continuum. Indeed, modernity itself is inexorably wedded to a global praxis of *chattel* slavery that generated specific structural-inert conditions of coloniality in the Raw that simultaneously attempt to reduce human 'being' to mere matter through objective violence, and then maintain this 'objecthood' as a perm-

---

[5] Douglass, p.218.

anent and 'natural' fact of life through miseducation of soul.

"To make a contented slave, you must make a thoughtless one. It is necessary to darken his moral and mental vision, and, as far as possible, to annihilate his power of reason. He must be able to detect no inconsistencies in slavery. The man that takes his earnings, must be able to convince him that he has a perfect right to do so. It must not depend upon mere force; the slave must know no Higher Law than his master's will. The whole relationship must not only demonstrate, to his mind, its necessity, but also its absolute rightfulness. If there be one crevice through which a single drop can fall, it will certainly rust away the slave's chain."[6] And yet a "contented slave" is not truly "thoughtless", even if it is only thoughts about self-preservation and pursuit of self-interest. For such thoughts serve to acclimate "slave" *identity* as an 'empirical self' well within the circumference of the Real as historically constituted by the normative gaze of western imperialist power that seeks to "annihilate his power of reason" towards maintaining "no Higher Law than his master's will". What Douglass means by *thought* is thus existentially weighted with an emancipatory relevance and intellectual rigor that breaches the passive reflexivity and "absolute rightfulness" of an everyday awareness predicated upon the violent systematic biopolitical pacification of human subjectivity which constitutes

---

[6] Frederick Douglass, *My Bondage and My Freedom*, (New York: Barnes and Noble Classics, 1855, 2005) p.238.

the "whole relationship" that imposes slavery upon human 'being' and yet "must not depend on mere force" alone. Therefore, to be "thoughtless" is to cede the emancipatory relevance of intellectual rigor to an informal logic of ordinary discourse that veils any "inconsistencies in slavery" as thoroughly as, and often in correlation with, the systematic formal rationality of the Academy.

As such, by intellectual rigor is not meant the mathematical rigor of the scientist who reifies formulaic experimental repetition towards utilitarian ends, or the rigor of logical analysis that retreats from the creative tension of enigma into the objective shelter of prescribed rules of thought that culminate in a reassuring clarity of epistemic closure.

Rather, what is meant by intellectual rigor is the intuitive questioning rigor of human 'being' enslaved and yet learning to read, write and interrogate the Real under constant threat of torture and death. The undaunted interpretive rigor of human 'being' as fugitive from the systematic imposition of *chattel* slavery, hermeneutically navigating through hostile environments while discerning emancipatory potentialities out of an entire constellation of everyday phenomena, when a sudden wrong interpretation leads not only to her own recapture, but to certain torture and death for all those brothers and sisters who wager their own freedom upon the rigorous fugitive pedagogy of the runaway slave as human 'being' escaping the social death of enslavement through the underground railroads of modernity towards a liberated horizon of human community.

insurgent philosophy in the Raw – Insurgent philosophy intervenes against the classical arrangement of thought between absolute claims of knowledge as set forth by scientific authority, absolute claims of truth as set forth by religious dogma and absolute claims of sovereign legitimacy as set forth by western imperialist power. As such, "Philosophy must go to school not only with the poets, philosophy needs to go to school with the musicians."[7]

Indeed, it is the responsibility of the philosopher to destabilize the melody of the absolute towards introducing stark staccato breakbeats of the possible, confronting the normative gaze and disrupting established structures of meaning, thereby enabling spontaneous potentialities of Truth to emerge out of the epistemic dissonance of interrogations of the Real and enunciations of Revolt. Philosophy as a sustained discursive engagement of rupture with unarticulated meaning, does not produce Truth and can never lay claim to possess Truth, but rather manifests a rugged commitment to an uninhibited search for a method of engagement with the revelation of Truth as it rises and sets upon the lived horizons of Religion, Science, Art, Love and Justice. It is this rigorous uninhibited search for Truth that allows philosophy to develop an epistemic rhythm towards its own possibility. Wright discloses the radical tempo of this insurgent philosophical rhythm, with his emancipatory discursive im-

---

[7] Cornel West, "Prophetic Fragments, Existential Blues", *The Brotherwise Dispatch*, Vol.2, Issue#23, March-May/2022.

perative to "be on top of theory; don't let theory be on top of you."[8]

The philosopher thus passionately seeks out and unsettles Truth wherever it is discursively wed into comfortable arrangements with established power, arousing lived potentialities and seducing Truth towards rupture from any coercive bonds of affinity with the normative gaze that restrain discursive potentialities from an emancipatory trajectory of dialectic engagement with the call of history and response of human subjectivity. Indeed, insurgent philosophical engagement enunciates Revolt at a register that is openly hostile to an imperial symphony of tradition, culture and institutional memory, thus interrogating the Real without deference to the normative gaze.

Insurgent philosophy takes a B-Boy stance facing forward as lived certitude of risk filled confrontational intentionality against a future without guarantees, back-to-back with "the Angel of history" whose "face is turned toward the past."[9] Indeed, "where *we* perceive a chain of events, *he* sees one single catastrophe, which keeps piling wreckage upon wreckage hurling it before his feet. The angel would like to stay, awaken the dead, and make whole what has been smashed." However, insurgent philosophy is no angel, and refuses to "stay" and "awaken the dead",

---

[8] Richard Wright, from *Black Power*, included in *Richard Wright Reader*, edited by Ellen Wright and Michel Fabre, (New York: Da Capo Press, 1997) p.107.
[9] Walter Benjamin, *Selected Writings Vol.4, 1938-1940*, (Cambridge, Mass: Belknap/Harvard Press, 2006) p.392.

precisely because awakening the dead cannot take place by staying behind, but rather by moving on ahead through emancipatory praxis that confronts the "storm" that "is blowing from Paradise" which "has got caught in" the "wings" of the Angel of history "with such violence the angel can no longer close them. This storm irresistibly propels him into the future to which his back is turned, while the pile of debris before him grows skyward." And yet, it is only by charging towards "*this storm*" that introduces the conditions of possibility for "what we call progress."[10]

Insurgent philosophy in the Raw begins as interrogations of the Real and enunciations of Revolt from the lived intensity of unfiltered proximity to the disaster of history, with an unapologetic orientation continuously tested by the socio-ontological weight of bearing witness to the global scope of human suffering, without the recuperative sentimentality Benjamin attributes to "the Angel of history" that seeks to "make whole what has been smashed". Although it is common to seek cultural nationalist respite in a mythic wholeness to be regained from a past shattered by catastrophe, how long can Black subjectivity avoid and seek to delay the lived universality constituted in confronting this disaster of coloniality head on through emancipatory praxis against Empire towards lived potentialities of geonational egalitarian community?

And yet, insurgent philosophy commits to the Blues metaphysic as a possibility of rebirth from

---

[10] ibid.

which to "awaken the dead", by introducing discursive openings towards emancipatory praxis and sustaining epistemic disequilibrium against a refined linear orchestra of accumulated traditions, dogmatic presuppositions and conventional wisdom. Insurgent philosophy then begins to reproach the continuous global reconfiguration of structural-inert violence that refurbishes this "pile of debris" under the veil of epistemological harmony with a western imperialist continuum.

As such, insurgent philosophy interrogates the Real and enunciates Revolt to the beat of discursive rhythms of thought that resonate outside the chords of a cognitive predictability that abuses scientific method, religious authority and cultural tradition as horizons of absolute truth and totality of knowledge intent on preserving epistemic closure under coercion from the normative gaze of established power.

Insurgent philosophy thus suffers equally under the impatient ridicule of 'common sense' advocacy, the metaphysical illusion of dogmatic religiosity and the formal rationality of academic sanction. For each exhibit an epistemological reliance upon an orthodox duality of thought intent on pacifying creative binary tensions by severing the medium of discourse from lived potentialities of the message it conveys. This analytical orientation appeases a pragmatic clarity of reductionist thought with a correlative promiscuity between necessary falsehood and attractive statistical findings as empirically meaningful, only the better to circumvent lived imperatives of insurgent philosophical method away from dialectical realization as an epistemic catalyst towards emancipatory praxis.

Conventional thought hence charts its success in commercial terms as tone-deaf objectivity based upon selling itself as a commodification of acquired knowledge at an inaudible distance from the Real. No doubt, reactionary efforts toward such cognitive distance reproduce thought as a commodity towards the renewal of objective registers of discursive commitment that demean and undermine the Blues metaphysic of lyrically dense layered imperatives of philosophical possibility over minimalist beats within close range and hence intimately coarse proximity to the Real.

To enunciate Revolt catalyzes thought through language towards disrupting the familiar continuity of the Real. Breakbeats of discontinuity from the lived topography of imperial coherence invigorate the philosophical trajectory of Black liberation discourse with an emancipatory relevance and intellectual rigor that confer merit upon thought through the insurgent caliber of its epistemic dissonance against the legitimating harmony of a western imperialist continuum. Thus, thought merits consideration as insurgent, in so far as it inscribes a lyrical constancy of intellectual rigor upon breakbeats of epistemic dissonance with emancipatory relevance as refusal of melodic approximation to the normative gaze.

Without an awareness of the emancipatory relevance of intellectual rigor as indispensable to the socio-historical narrative of human liberation that conditions lived Black experience towards an opening, a possibility – *a way out of no way* – since the imposition of modernity by western imperialist power, it becomes that much easier to uncritically succumb to the normative gaze which legitimizes what Cruse condemns as the "fundamentally anti-theoretical, anti-aesthetic, anti-cultural, anti-intellectual . . . application of values in the pursuit of materialistic ends."[11] Indeed, insurgent philosophy rejects such sound pragmatic injunctions that dull the cutting edge of Black liberation discourse into an accessible language of informal logic tailored to non-resisting masses already mercilessly conditioned to approach thought as yet another market oriented commodity.

To enunciate Revolt dislocates Truth from its stable firmament within an imperial constellation and traces its once celestial trajectory of veracity, thus coming to terms with its violent structural positionality and newfound relativity within that "pile of debris" as readily visible to dogmatic regulations of thought unearthed in archaeological fashion by sifting through the epistemic ruins of authority leaning upon the weathered pillars of science and religion to stabilize the lived topography of its own socio-historical coherence. As such, the normative gaze coerces Truth into an impossible stability that deliberately exiles Truth from the Real, the better to further obfuscate the source of its sovereign legitimacy by the very propagation of objective violence and miseducation of

---

[11] Harold Cruse, *Crisis of the Negro Intellectual*, (New York: Apollo Editions, 1967) p.100.

soul that imposes an unreflective fealty unto itself as absolute authority in the absence of Truth that it necessarily veils by the sheer volume of its dogmatic claims.

Empire anchors its epistemic cartography as the Real through coloniality of power at the expense of Truth. When no longer visible as a dialectic rupture in the sky of the Divine, the emergence of Truth into the Real of history thus becomes contingent upon emancipatory praxis. To be sure, emancipatory praxis does not itself create Truth, but rather introduces the conditions of possibility for its emergence upon the horizon of lived experience as Religion, Science, Art, Love or Justice against the normative gaze of a western imperialist continuum. No philosophy, worthy of the name, dismisses the ardor of search or reasons away the risk of undertaking required of human 'being' when encountering Truth. Indeed, insurgent philosophy compels one to seek Truth even where it leads to messianic Revelation in a Persian dungeon or messianic Revolt against human slavery throughout the Americas.

Indeed, Black liberation discourse discloses enunciations of Revolt towards lived potentialities of emancipatory praxis under even the harshest of socio-historical circumstances by virtue of its genesis through existential resistance against the systematic biopolitical imposition of *chattel* slavery upon human 'being'.

Thus, the insurgent philosophical discourse of Black liberation incites interrogations of the Real without ceding sovereign legitimacy to a western imperialist continuum. Cleaver understood this far too well. "For too long Black people have *relied* upon the analyses and ideological perspectives of others. Our struggle has reached a point now where it would be absolutely suicidal for us to continue this *posture of dependency*. No other people in the world are in the same position as we are, and no other people in the world can get us out of it except ourselves. There are those who are all too willing to do our thinking for us, even if it gets us killed. However, they are not willing to follow through and do our dying for us. If thoughts bring about our deaths, let them at least be our own thoughts, so that we will have broken, once and for all, with the flunkeyism of dying for every cause and every error – except our own."[12] Remembering always that it is precisely due to the geohistorical significance of the fact that "no other people in the world are in the same *position* as we are" that Black liberation constitutes the universal scope of its emancipatory relevance.

And yet, in movement towards constituting sociohistorically relevant enunciations of Revolt, no self-respecting Black radical intellectual refuses to *engage* with "the analyses and ideological perspectives of others". The insurgent trajectory of Cleaver's own thought contributes towards the theoretical basis for the Black Panther Party's unrivaled revolutionary

---

[12] Eldridge Cleaver, "On the Ideology of the Black Panther Party", *Target Zero*, (New York: Palgrave Macmillan, 1969, 2006) p.172. emphasis mine.

internationalist orientation and working non-paternalistic solidarity with the New Left.[13] As such, it is *reliance* on the normative gaze of a western imperialist continuum towards bestowing epistemic legitimacy upon insurgent thought that Cleaver stridently warns against.

Insurgent philosophical discourse is characterized by interrogating the Real and enunciating Revolt towards generating epistemic ruptures between thought and the easy familiarity of self-evident imperial consensus. "This raises a crucial question as to whether members of the established white American radical movement would even recognize a new radical theory if they saw it. This is especially true when and if such a new radical theory emanates from the Black direction."[14] Indeed, radical theory emanating from the socio-ontological underground of modernity as "the Black direction", does not speak in oppositional idioms of civil society vying for reconciliation within and recognition from the imperial mainstream. Rather "the Black direction" of thought, disrupts the imperial coherence of modernity itself by voicing an exceptional antagonism that discloses its irreconcilable trajectory of emancipatory praxis against western imperialist power.

---

[13] Cleaver, *Soul on Ice*, (New York: Delta/Dell Publishing, 1968, 1991) and *Post-Prison Writings & Speeches*, (New York: Vintage, 1969). Joshua Bloom and Waldo E. Martin Jr., *Black Against Empire*, (Berkeley: University of California Press, 2013).
[14] Harold Cruse, *Rebellion or Revolution*, (New York: William Morrow & Company, 1968) p.27.

Unfamiliar ideas and conceptual difficulties arise from interrogating the exceptional antagonism of lived Black experience, thus provoking unfamiliar thoughts and difficult questions in relation to the Real that revoke the epistemological sanctity of the normative gaze, all in favor of a lived insecurity of spiritual anxiety and dread that unveils the possibility of intellectual growth at the expense of unreflective culture and popular consensus guaranteed by miseducation of soul and objective violence.

How is it possible then, to expect Black liberation discourse to be so easily susceptible to passive comprehension when it consists of destabilizing a formal logic that stubbornly recognizes its own possibility as the result of deterministic replications predicated upon fixed constellations of imperial coherence? For as Wright tellingly enunciates, "And at the moment this process starts, at the moment when a people begin to realize a meaning in their suffering, the civilization that engenders that suffering is doomed."[15] No doubt, Black liberation exerts an unbearable socio-ontological weight of emancipatory dissonance upon ordinary discourse and formal logic, unsettling an entire coloniality of reference that posits itself as epistemologically exhaustive and in complete harmony with the Real.

Indeed, the discursive movement of Black liberation against the normative gaze constitutes an eman-

---

[15] Richard Wright, "Blueprint for Negro Writing", *Richard Wright Reader*, p.41.

cipatory rhythm of insurgent philosophy between increasing epistemic proximity to the Real, socio-ontological disequilibrium and historical gravity of unavoidable confrontation against Empire.

As an insurgent philosophical enunciation of Revolt, Black liberation discourse does not correspond to a melodic epistemological synchronicity with the Real, but rather opens potentialities of rupture against the Real through its very interrogation, and as such cannot be enunciated authentically within the normative gaze without calling modernity itself, as imposed by western imperialist power, fundamentally into question.

Academics, typical readers and insurgent philosophy – In response to sequestering all philosophical endeavor within formal rationality as sanctioned Academic thought, insurgent philosophy deliberately resists the dogmatic presupposition that firm adherence to an analytical logic, which develops linearly towards a well foreseen conclusion, is the absolute hallmark of intellectual rigor. Such epistemic coercion aids in pacifying the intentionality of insurgent thought by brutally policing the Black radical imagination until its very structure facilitates the laundering of emancipatory potentialities into a merely oppositional equilibrium within the normative gaze of established power.

Indeed, in anticipation of potentialities towards the existential refraction of Black liberation discourse into emancipatory praxis, insurgent philosophy unceremoniously ruptures the overdetermined coordination of thought as dissolved into specialized disciplines upheld by institutional watchdogs as the boundaries of reason itself.

As such, and in spite of any well-meaning encouragement to dilute the confrontationally enigmatic and often fragmentary style of conceptually dense thoroughgoing critique that characterizes the discursive intensity of insurgent philosophical prose, there is no inherent epistemic value in allowing Black liberation discourse to be regulated in advance of the emancipatory trajectory of thinking itself, especially without regard to the purpose such thought is directed towards and whatever adversity such thought is meant to overcome. "The appeal to science, the rules by which it functions, the absolute validity of the methods to which it owes its development, together constitute an authority which penalizes free, untrammeled, 'untrained' thinking, and will not allow the minds of men to dwell on matters that do not bear the stamp of its approval. Science, the means to autonomy, has degenerated into an instrument of heteronomy."[16] In this sense, we must resist authorizing the scientific merit of systematic thought when it epistemologically forestalls the interrogative freedom of interpretative rigor.

Therefore, insurgent philosophy revels in a refusal to exercise any discursive leniency upon either academics or so-called typical readers, for it necessarily demands acute levels of concentration from the reader towards dispensing with settling for either an *academic* or a *typical* understanding of our contemporary world. Or are we now expected to believe that western imperialist power has no vested socio-historical interest in ideologically maintaining the intellectual fidelity of academics who aid in manufacturing consent while simultaneously orchestrating the ideological stabilization of everyday people as common sense and conventional wisdom?

No doubt, in the critical cultivation of philosophical disdain for what is often described as 'the typical reader', do we not hear philosophy itself grappling with its own overdetermination-from-without based

---

[16] Theodor Adorno, "Why Philosophy?", *The Adorno Reader* edited by Brian O'Connor, (Malden, MA: Blackwell Publishing, 2000) p.49.

on pedestrian standards of language and logical regulations of analytic thought that perhaps apply to good journalism, effective activism and/or equally sound pedagogy, but fall short of approaching the inhospitable summits of insurgent philosophical endeavor? "Thought has allowed itself to become, as it were, intimidated, and no longer possesses the self-confidence to go beyond the mere reproduction of what is anyway."[17] When philosophy overrides its discursive orientation towards Truth with a pragmatic concern for reaching 'the typical reader', are we supposed to feign surprise at the debasement of Black liberation discourse imprisoned in *typical* books, written in *typical* language, meant to convey *typical* outlooks that cultivate a *typical* relation to established power ie. unreflective subservient complicity?

And yet, as difficult as it is to find thinkers within the Academy, and let us be fair in admitting that enough do in fact exist, who write with emancipatory relevance and epistemic freedom from disciplinary constraints, financial incentives, careerist considerations and imperial mainstream prestige, it is even more difficult to find thinkers outside of the Academy who don't pander to thought at its lowest common denominator in the name of vain cultural nationalist attempts to reach the dominated non-resisting masses by humbly indulging popular culture on its own self-aggrandizing terms of success, and thus by default

---

[17] Adorno, p.51.

epistemologically capitulate to the normative gaze of Empire.

The normative gaze inundates both academic thought and typical thinking with an unarticulated deference to formal rationality and established structures of meaning, at the expense of epistemic movement towards interrogations of the Real and enunciations of Revolt.

As such, insurgent philosophy introduces disequilibrium within the very epistemic coherence of philosophy as a specialized academic discipline and ruptures its legitimating authorization of the normative gaze into formal rationality being passed down from generation to generation as *typical* thought within a tradition. Under such conditions, philosophy strains to recognize itself outside the simulacrum of its own obituary as ghostwritten by the Academy after an incessantly Nietzschean funeral for metaphysics replete with a eulogy that as a consequence proclaims the 'end of philosophy' by its evolution and dispersal into the independent sciences as academic disciplines.[18]

However, insurgent philosophy shares its radical beginnings with the Blues metaphysic, as a rejection of the very premise of such a funeral, and thus opens epistemic potentialities for the rebirth of philosophy itself, to the frustration of Academics, by introducing conditions of possibility for transcending the reifi-

---

[18] Martin Heidegger, "The End of Philosophy and the Task of Thinking", *Basic Writings*, (New York: HarperCollins, 1977, 1993) pp.431-449.

cation of specialized disciplines towards more socially relevant modes of intellectual engagement.

Insurgent philosophy – even at its most basic – is not the kind of thought that appeases academics or 'the typical reader'. For insurgent philosophy exerts demands upon the reader, who then, in overcoming any discursive intimidation through close difficult readings, begins to experience an understanding of the Real that ceases to be *academic* or *typical*.

As such, let there be no talk of a retreat from indispensable dialogue with everyday people or the Academy. Black liberation discourse, in venturing forth unremittingly from the socio-ontological underground of modernity, confronts the normative gaze of a western imperialist continuum without need of established structures of meaning as its epistemic foundation, save for the trajectory of its own discursive movement towards emancipatory praxis. Insurgent philosophy channels the exceptional antagonism of lived Black experience and discursively disrupts the geohistorical equilibrium that conceals the universality of human 'being', thus revealing the Blues metaphysic as a vast reservoir of socio-ontological Revolt that allows the emancipatory intentionality of Black liberation discourse to constitute and legitimate the necessary rigors of thought, and not the other way around.

Critical Encounters

being-in-the-world and Coates – Even for radical autonomous intellectual brothers deliberately cultivating a peripheral relation to mainstream media for insurgent potentialities against sanctioned purveyors of imperialist structures of meaning, it has been impossible to ignore each wave of accolades surrounding Ta-Nehisi Coates' *Between the World and Me*[19] since its publication. Of course, it doesn't hurt Coates' chances of renown by paying his literary dues at *The Village Voice* and *The Atlantic*, though even a brief perusal of Coates' work is enough to realize that he is not just another wannabe posing as a writer long enough to enjoy the spoils of punditry and 'experthood'. Coates' prose reveals a rare wholehearted engagement with writing as a singular and demanding mode of 'being-in-the-world'.

Therefore, instead of holding Coates accountable for media hype originating in the disinterested smell of collaborationists, reeking of stale cheese, wine and privilege emanating from within a 'white' cultural nationalist discourse of 'fixed' parameters, yet open to a lively hyperbourgeois herd of liberal and conservative intelligentsia who valiantly adhere to an American exceptionalism, and as such, carefully cultivate the type of close ties to established power such principled ideological deference to Empire allows; lets delve into the theoretical implications drawn from Coates' contributions as an emerging progressive Black fugitive literary voice within an often irrelevant and dated nat-

---

[19] Ta-Nehisi Coates, *Between The World And Me*, (New York: Spiegel & Grau, 2015).

ional public discourse surrounding 'race' and its relation to a western imperialist continuum. Indeed, what is it about this work, which is generating such unencumbered literary buzz at this crucial socio-historical juncture?

Between the World and Me arrives as long ignored emancipatory imperatives for social justice are reawakening and challenging the historical quiet and sovereign legitimacy of Empire, as the world again bears witness to an ascendant humanity in spontaneous rebellion sparked by neo-colonial police murder in places like Ferguson, Missouri and Baltimore, Maryland. As such, the objective violence against human 'being' inscribed in modernity by western imperialist power is Returning to source with greater and greater frequency as insurrection-in-itself.

The assertion of Black subjectivity-as-human 'being' exerts an exceptional antagonistic resonance against the structural-inert violence of modernity, stimulating a dynamic and growing grassroots flow of social activist formations and broad-based oppositional coalitions emerging around the tragic singularities of lived Black experience. Indeed, the Raw coloniality of lived Black experience discloses the Real of the human condition *overdetermined-from-without* by western imperialist power. Not out of some chauvinistic 'racial' essentialism, which often functions as a nascent stage of dialectic awakening towards even more mature emancipatory implications of lived Black experience, but rather, because our 'being-in-the-world' is historically situated within the normative gaze of modernity as a social pathology and ontological 'problem', and thus constitutes an exceptional antagonism with inhospitable destabilizing consequences in relation to established power and imperial structures of meaning that sustain the status quo.

Building upon the *anti-slavery dialectic* of Frederick Douglass, W.E.B. DuBois initiates another poignant philosophical formulation of this exceptional antagonism in his seminal classic, *The Souls of Black Folk*, by way of a single question: "how does it feel to be a problem?" *Between the World and Me* is Coates' sincere literary attempt to convey the historical magnitude and existential severity of this perpetual question of lived Black experience to his 14-year-old son in the form of a letter. "I tell you now that the question of how one should live within a black body, within a country lost in the Dream, is the question of my life, and the pursuit of this question, I have found, ultimately answers itself." This reformulation by Coates contains an epistemological impetus which permeates the scope of his writings.

Indeed, Coates' reformulation "ultimately answers itself" as 'the beautiful struggle' of survival, self-discovery and somehow ultimately escaping the specificities of structural-inert racist dehumanization he faced while growing up in Baltimore. "Before I could discover, before I could escape, I had to survive, and this could only mean a clash with the streets". Amidst discovery, flight, and survival, what's missing is any enunciation or desire which might have been expressed as 'before I could fight back'. Coates' writings disclose a progressive Black fugitive literary engagement in movement *away* from an all too pervasive socio-historical oppression. Indeed, in relation to established structures of power, he is no collaborationist thinker like Stanley Crouch or John McWhorter, and in this there is much to respect. However, brothers and sisters seeking a more emancipatory engagement of intellectual endeavor *against* oppression should look elsewhere. That "clash with the streets" never elevates into a confrontation, intellectual or otherwise, with Empire. "But part of what I know is that there is the burden of living among Dreamers, and there is the extra burden of your country telling you the Dream is just, noble, and real, and you are crazy for seeing the corruption and smelling the sulfur. For their innocence, they nullify your anger, your fear, until you are coming and going, and you find yourself inveighing against yourself – 'Black people are the only people who . . .' – really inveighing against your own humanity and raging against the crime in your ghetto, because you are powerless before the great crime of history that brought the ghettos to be."

Clearly, Coates builds a formidable case for the necessity of an existence open to so much more than mere surviving on the run, only to discursively drown emancipatory potentialities within a deliberate ambiguity that conflates any distinction between survival and liberation, thus suppressing questions of freedom by off-handedly dismissing the dynamic correlation between human agency and emancipatory praxis. So, even though "it is truly horrible to understand yourself as the essential below of your country", Coates refuses to articulate an imperative of struggle *against* oppression relevant to the socio-ontological underground of modernity, whom he accurately refers to as "the essential below", leaving us instead with a "struggle to understand" oppression as "our only advantage over this madness". Word? . . . "only advantage"? The imperial mainstream rejoices as the underground of modernity continues to suffer in puzzled lament.

Aiding in this suppression of questions of freedom is a conceptual overreliance on "the body" littered throughout the book, thus promoting a continued reification of lived Black experience as 'objecthood' which began with systematic violence intent on reducing human 'being' to matter through *chattel* slavery. Coates fails to make the epistemological connection between "the premise that allows for these killing fields – the reduction of the black body", and the reduction of Black subjectivity-as-human 'being' to 'the body' in his own literary endeavors. At times, even Fanon employs a decolonizing phenomenological discourse that situates 'the body' within imperialist structures of meaning as an opening towards questions of human subjectivity. However, when Coates clumsily appropriates this same vocabulary, it has the opposite effect of aligning his work with the normative gaze of modernity through a vulgar logical positivist reduction of "the spirit and soul" to "the body and brain", thus inducing what Lewis R. Gordon conceptualizes as 'epistemic closure'.[20]

Although this use by Coates of 'the body' works extremely well as a discursive maneuver within the confines of stressing the sheer "visceral experience" that situates Black subjectivity as human 'being-in-the-world' in this letter to his son, it doesn't quite hold up under the weight of insurgent philosophical scrutiny. "And by what miracle is the materialist, who accuses idealists of indulging in metaphysics when they reduce matter to mind, absolved from the same charge when he reduces mind to matter? Experience does not decide in favor of his doctrine – nor, for that matter, does it decide in favor of the opposing one either. Experience is confined to displaying the close connection between the physiological and the psychological, and this connection is subject to a thousand different kinds of interpretation."[21]

---

[20] "Epistemic closure is a moment of presumably complete knowledge of a phenomenon. Such presumed knowledge closes off efforts at further inquiry." Lewis R. Gordon, *What Fanon Said*, (New York: Fordam University Press, 2015) p.49.

[21] Sartre continues pulling no punches - "The principles of materialism seem philosophically false, how could matter give rise to the idea of matter? . . . It seems as though its first step is to deny the existence of God and transcendent finality; second, to reduce the action of mind to that of matter; third, to eliminate subjectivity by reducing the world, and man in it, to a system of objects linked together by universal relationships. I conclude in good faith that it is a metaphysical doctrine and that materialists are metaphysicians. ... Materialism is a metaphysics hiding positivism; but it is a self-destructive metaphysics, for by undermining metaphysics out of principle, it deprives its own statements of any foundation. . . . The materialist . . . leaves

Now, despite the fact that deciding to write in letter format is an obvious nod to Baldwin's aesthetic influence, embracing such a popular literary device in an era discursively flooded with self-help jargon and therapeutic accommodationist paradigms is probably not an uninformed market strategy ultimately catering to the spiritual dross afflicting the *imperial mainstream*, rather than the emancipatory needs of the socio-ontological *underground of modernity*. Still, unlike his contemporaries, Coates thrives in the epistolary genre, easily surpassing the blunt mendacity of Sam Harris' *Letter to a Christian Nation* and Hill Harper's

---

behind him science and subjectivity and the human and substitutes himself for God, Whom he denies, in order to contemplate the spectacle of the universe. . . . 'The materialist conception of the world means simply the conception of nature as it is, without anything foreign added.' What is involved in this surprising text is the elimination of human subjectivity, 'that addition foreign to nature.' The materialist thinks that by denying subjectivity he has made it disappear. But the trick is easy to expose. In order to eliminate subjectivity, the materialist declares that he is an object, that is, the subject matter of science. But once he has eliminated subjectivity in favor of the object, instead of seeing himself as a thing among things, buffeted about by the physical universe, he makes of himself an objective beholder and claims to contemplate nature as it is, in the absolute. There is a play on words objectivity, which sometimes means the passive quality of the object beheld and, at other times, the absolute value of a beholder stripped of subjective weaknesses. Thus having transcended all subjectivity and identified himself with pure objective truth, the materialist travels about in a world of objects inhabited by human objects. . . . Materialism makes a certainty of what appears to us to be a rash induction, or, if you prefer, a postulate." – Jean-Paul Sartre, "Materialism and Revolution," *Literary and Philosophical Essays*, (New York: Collier Books, 1955) p.199-202.

trilogy of banality: *Letters to a Young Brother, Letters to a Young Sister and Letters to an Incarcerated Brother*, with a tremendous literary acumen that indeed merits substantive comparison to Baldwin for subjecting "our country to an exceptional moral standard. This is difficult because there exists all around us, an apparatus urging us to accept American innocence at face value and not to inquire too much." And yet, the same morally reprimanding harshness he wields against "the Believers" and "the Dreamers" throughout the book, effectively allows for his thoughts to become yet another mode of easily digestible nonconformism[22] for imperial hyperbourgeois appetites as emotional catharsis, precisely because his writings are permeated with historical indictment bereft of emancipatory imperative. Thus, leaving the "apparatus" blemished, but fundamentally unchallenged.

Baldwin's profound moralist suasion harnesses an uncanny capacity for awakening readers to a renewed sense of human agency arising from the unsettling truth that "there is simply no possibility of a real change in the Negro's situation without the most radical and far-reaching changes in American political and social

---

[22] "They had much to be rebellious about, but found it extremely difficult to be "revolutionary" against the bourgeois Establishment. Theirs was a revolt in terms of aesthetics, sex, interracialism, life-styles, the cult of the material medica of narcotic elixirs, the movement of "beat" spirituality, etc. all of which were the ingredients of non-conformism, American style."
– Harold Cruse, *Rebellion or Revolution*, (New York: William Morrow & Company, 1968) p.174.

structure."²³ Coates also summons the Black radical imagination with compelling force; "there is nothing uniquely evil in these destroyers or even in this moment. The destroyers are merely men enforcing the whims of our country, correctly interpreting its heritage and legacy". Consequently, any potentialities of emancipatory thought, are suffocated by the Absurd vacillation between somehow accepting "the chaos of history", even when acknowledging lived Black experience as "the clearest evidence America is indeed the work of men".

Indeed, if "what matters is the system that makes your body breakable" then why naturalize western imperialist power as an "earthquake" that "cannot be subpoenaed" or compare the neo-colonial police officer who murdered his college friend Prince Jones to a "force of nature, the helpless agent of our world's physical laws"? Such a comparison facilitates an abdication of human subjectivity based upon the realization of how Absurd it must then be to resist neo-colonial police violence as the very embodiment of "our world's physical laws". And yet, since Coates "could not retreat, as did so many, into the church and its mysteries", what then justifies his "retreat" into materialist determinism "and its mysteries"? Retreat, my brother, is still retreat.

As such, Baldwin's penchant for "speaking of political freedom in spiritual terms",²⁴ is thoroughly

---

[23] James Baldwin, "Down at the Cross", *Collected Essays*, (New York: Library of America, 1962, 1998) p.335.
[24] Baldwin, p.337.

mishandled by Coates' ability to speak of socio-historical oppression in terms of physics, biology and "all the matter floating through the cosmos". In this sense, Coates is temporarily betrayed by his own atheist temperament that is actually refreshing when focused on the outright rejection of "magic in all its forms", including a sound critique of the magical imperialist cult of good individual intentions that somehow influences the world unmediated by the structural constraints of established power: "it does not matter that the 'intentions' of individual educators were noble. Forget about intentions. What any institution, or its agents, 'intend' for you is secondary. Our world is physical. Learn to play defense – ignore the head and keep your eyes on the body. Very few Americans will directly proclaim that they are in favor of black people being left to the streets. But a very large number of Americans will do all they can to preserve the Dream."

The ultimate strength of Coates' writing is that he creatively delves into our 'problematic' lived Black experience with enough tacit progressive literary poise, as to have actually touched a nerve amongst the imperial mainstream by sustaining a misguided dualism that posits survival and liberation as concrete opposites. Sound prose draws the reader into a movingly truthful narrative conveying intimate emotional intricacies of ongoing oppression against human 'being', while painstakingly preserving a non-confrontational discursive trajectory with regards to Empire. With all the historical evidence of structural-inert oppression at Coates's disposal throughout the book, this is seriously no small feat. Why else would Toni Morrison state in good conscience that Coates fills "the intellectual void that plagued me after James Baldwin died"? Has anyone else since Baldwin displaced emancipatory critique of structural-inert violence with such trenchant affective integrity? Or have we forgotten that it was Baldwin, who when confronted with the insurgent intellectual endeavors of DuBois,[25] Wright, Fanon and Cesaire at the 1956 Pan-African Writers Conference in Paris, France no less, actually wrote that it has "never been in our interest" to overthrow the "machinery of the oppressor"?[26] Word? ... "never"?

Much like Baldwin, Coates is often mistakenly painted as a Black radical thinker by neo-conservative eunuchs who enjoy their 'white bread' cultural nationalist American exceptionalism untainted by historical truth. Framing the intensely welcome response to Coates' work as a new wave of 'radical chic' is insincere, and clearly a proven strategic rhetorical maneuver meant not only to deter social discourse about 'race' from gaining any emancipatory traction, but also intended to siphon the intellectual legitimacy of any burgeoning radical aspirations of solidarity among youth of all socio-cultural backgrounds who are

---

[25] Though actually barred from attending in person due to western imperialist intrigue, DuBois addressed the conference through a letter read on his behalf.
[26] Baldwin, "Princes and Powers", p.148.

justifiably dissatisfied with the status quo. Indeed, yet another generation is beginning to discover the difference between *protest-as-ritual event* and *protest-as-resistance* in places like the streets of Coates' own Baltimore.

The sublime lived experience of postmodern lumpenproletariat brothers and sisters in Baltimore actualizing an insurgent unity by exercising human agency in refusing to yield to the tyranny of neo-colonial police agents, throwing rocks and boulders at the consistent perpetrators of objective violence against the ascendant humanity of Black community, offers a stark contrast to the narrative of stifling "fear" Coates projects onto his own hometown. Such is the implicated condition of our temporality as human 'being'; history rarely fails to overwhelm the pen.

Coates if you scared, say you scared. "And I am afraid". Fair enough. However, such ruthless interrogation of "the subject that elicited the most sympathy and rationalizing – myself" obviously failed to alleviate his own "fear", thus prompting Coates to project this "fear" upon the Black community he grew up around. "But I was afraid long before you, and in this I was unoriginal. When I was your age, the only people I knew were black, and all of them were powerfully, adamantly and dangerously afraid. I had seen this fear all my young life, though I had not always recognized it as such." This questionable projection of paralyzing "fear" upon Black community is indistinguishable from the normative gaze of modernity that demeans our socio-ontological potentialities and historical capacity for human agency towards upheaval against western imperialist power.

And yet, might Coates have misread dread as fear? Surely, he already admitted about fear that "I had not always recognized it as such". Still, even if we cede the point to Coates that indeed fear consumed "all of them": might what is fear today, become dread tomorrow? For although fear ensues as an outward emotionally direct correspondence to the unknown; dread arises as an emotional mediation of interiority confronting the unknown through reflexive interrogation of potentialities for human agency. Fear is the awareness of Sandra Bland being pulled over for a minor traffic violation, that this routine stop might be the death of her. Dread is the recognition by Sandra Bland, that whether she is polite or rude, whether she cooperates or resists, she might die either way, but must still inevitably decide her course of action in the face of such comprehensive ambiguity.

No Black community is unfamiliar with the objective violence, economic subjugation, and miseducation of soul that exact such an effective *biopolitical pacification* upon human 'being'. As such, the Raw coloniality of established power is not an unknown factor, for it situates lived Black experience, its tension is palpable, the hunger it inflicts upon human 'being' is tangible, its suffocation of human subjectivity is rote, and it is the very condition of possibility for the historical triumph of modernity. The normative gaze of a western imperialist continuum enforces a coercive anonymity upon the ascendant humanity of

Black community. Hence, consciousness of our lived potentialities towards asserting Black subjectivity-as-human 'being' in the face of such coercive anonymity is experienced as dread. Dread is the conscious apprehension of existential freedom facing the inevitability of socio-historical persecution. "In America, it is traditional to destroy the black body – *it is heritage.*" Dread accompanies our presence towards self, engagement in the world and intersubjective resonance towards one another, in our attempts to overcome the reign of *double consciousness*, pitting an intimate reflexive awareness of human 'being' against the normative gaze of established power that overdetermines lived Black experience into 'objecthood', precisely because the assertion of Black subjectivity-as-human 'being' against a globalized structural-inert oppression makes us even more vulnerable to gratuitous "disembodiment".

In spite of, and maybe even because of the way Coates interprets his father's radical past, Coates is not himself an insurgent thinker laying siege to imperialist structures of meaning in an intellectual melee for the highest stakes. "Dad believed in revolution, but the truth is, he was always eminently suited to the world as it was . . . He thought his country was rotten, but he was a better fit than he knew."[27] Coates chooses to understand his father's intellectual pursuits as at odds with "revolution", instead of realizing the

---

[27] Ta-Nehisi Coates, *The Beautiful Struggle*, (New York: Spiegel & Grau, 2009) p.81-2.

depth of revolutionary continuity disclosed by such insurgent intellectual endeavor as emancipatory praxis. However, for someone whose own immediate and extended family were among that countless, forgotten and precious humanity on the receiving end of a pervasive counterinsurgent blow-back by western imperialist power against the Black Panther Party, that's his call to make.

As such, Coates constitutes his fugitive intellectual engagement as a contemporary moral sentinel, befittingly atheist enough for such an impossible yet inevitable task, trenchantly admonishing anyone who "would rather live white than live free" that their "forgetting is a habit, yet another component of the Dream. They have forgotten the scale of theft that enriched them in slavery; the terror that allowed them, for a century, to pilfer the vote; the segregationist policy that gave them their suburbs." Such literary efforts, no matter how limited in scope, are a welcome assistance to, though they can never substitute for, a more insurgent trajectory against the normative gaze of established power. Indeed, Coates is that rare brother who can intellectually regulate neo-conservative eunuchs like David Brooks and Andrew Sullivan on their own home turf, and more importantly, in a way that weakens them in front of their own constituency – the imperial mainstream.

Coates' Black progressive dissent is urgent, studied and vibrant. And yet, the range of his theoretical limitations betrays a discursive reliance on an epistemological arrangement that veils the constant and varied reconfigurations of western imperialist power as unintelligible and chaotic, unavoidably mystifying the competent, deliberate and extremely efficient social, economic and historical ordering of the world according to the racist dehumanizing precepts of Empire and coloniality.

oppositional thought after the fall – As a significant study and measured intellectual history of Marxist theory and socialist discourse bleeding out of mainstream Leftist journals in response to the geopolitical collapse of the Soviet Union and the subsequent demise of the Eastern Bloc, *Intellectual Radicalism After 1989* [28] clinically refuses to indulge in any grand pronouncements akin to Francis Fukiyama's infamous claim of the 'end of history'.[29] Instead, Sebastian Berg exhibits an analytical temperament of numbing glacial objectivity, as he tediously mines a vast array of epistemological tensions and political apologetics engaged in by the mainstream Left to account for its historic failure at consummating and sustaining an authentic socialist political project within Western Europe or the United States.

To be clear, the value of this work lies not in its novelty, but rather in Berg's remarkable achievement of meticulously cataloging oppositional thought, as exemplified and filtered through the political orientations and theoretical trajectories of *New Left Review* and *Socialist Register* in Great Britain and *Monthly Review* and *Dissent* in the United States, against the globalized tide of advanced neo-liberal capitalist hegemony.

---

[28] Sebastian Berg, *Intellectual Radicalism After 1989*, (Bielefeld, Germany: Transcipt Verlag, 2016).
[29] Francis Fukiyama, *The End of History and The Last Man*, (New York: Avon Books, 1992).

However, Berg is extremely careful in refusing to confront the historical crisis of orthodox Leftist perspectives he surveys head on. Rather, his prose discloses a deconstructive methodology which, "considering the narrative intention of the texts, it nevertheless reads them with questions in mind that are in many cases different from the questions the writers addressed in their articles and from the purposes their texts served". This strategy has the effect, desired or not, of allowing the editorial decisions and theoretical preoccupations of such notable figures like Irving Howe, Paul Sweezy, Perry Anderson and Ralph Miliband, to ultimately contribute towards a quieting condemnation of whatever combined vestiges of Marxist theory and socialist democracy they still creatively endorsed in the immediate aftermath of the political dissolution of Soviet style nation-state communism in 1989.

Of key importance to understanding the scope of this work is a fundamental paradox introduced into Leftist thought by the failed project of Soviet communism in particular, to radical orientations existing in Western Europe and the United States. For as Berg asserts, "this constitutes a paradox because Western Marxism in most of its shades had for a long time distanced itself from really existing socialism". Indeed, can anyone really dispute that Western Marxism had been at least consistently critical, if not openly hostile to "really existing socialism", be it manifest in closed social formations of Eastern Europe or within open social formations of the imperial mainstream in Western metropoles?

As such, Berg's study presents enough evidentiary momentum towards suggesting that the geopolitical trajectory of socialist projects themselves lent even more historical credence to a discursive abandonment of once untouchable dogmatic pillars of Marxist theory. The lived implausibility of economic determinism, dialectical materialism and blind messianic faith in the working class as the singular motor of linear historical progress, thus fueled Post-Marxism as poststructuralist inflected discursive reconfigurations that ultimately obscure if not completely abandon such blatant theoretical vulnerabilities of Marxist thought.

What eventually comes to the fore however, is a disconcerting geopolitical complicity of Marxism, which though in historical opposition to capital, finds itself alarmingly at peace with Empire. Or as Marx himself discloses, "in fact the veiled slavery of the wage labourers in Europe needed the unqualified slavery of the New World as its pedestal."[30]

As such, fundamental to this Post-Marxist orientation is a quietist resignation to the parliamentary democratic simulacrum of a civil society that is predicated upon racist dehumanization and coloniality.[31]

---

[30] Karl Marx, *Capital Vol.1*, (New York: Penguin Classics, 1867, 1990) p.925.
[31] Anibal Quijano, "Coloniality of Power, Eurocentrism and Latin America", included in *Coloniality at Large*, edited by Mabel

As Berg's work notably documents, "Marxism's anti-imperialist internationalism has been replaced by an acceptance of the capitalist world system which again can only be changed incrementally." Post-Marxism thus indulges in a cathartic liberal disavowal of the revolutionary human agency required to overthrow unjust structural-inert power, as inherently totalitarian. Of course, then "it follows from this approach that the traditional Marxist conception of revolution has run its course."

Never the less, a question arises that perhaps even troubles the astute reader. In what sense then, can such contemporary orientations of Marxism still be considered radical? Or if we are to take DuBois[32] seriously, or even Foucault,[33] just how radical was

---

Morana, Enrique Dussel, and Carlos A. Juaregui, (Durham, NC: Duke University Press, 2008) pp.181-224.

[32] "Modern imperialism and modern industrialism are one and the same system; root and branch of the same tree. The race problem is the *other side* of labor problem; . . . remembering always that *empire* is the heavy hand of capital abroad . . . this almost naïve setting of the darker races beyond the pale of democracy and of modern humanity . . . involves two things – acquiescence of the darker peoples and agreement between capital and labor in white democracies." W.E.B. DuBois, "The Negro Mind Reaches Out", included in *The New Negro*, edited by Alain Locke, (New York: Touchstone Book, 1925, 1992) pp.386 & 402. Emphasis mine.

[33] "At the deepest level of Western knowledge, Marxism introduced no real discontinuity; it found its place without difficulty, as a full, quiet, comfortable and, goodness knows, satisfying form for a time (its own), within an epistemological arrangement that welcomed it gladly (since it was this arrangement that was in fact making room for it) and that it, in return, had no intention of disturbing and, above all, no power to modify, even one jot, since

Marxism itself in relation to modernity as imposed by western imperialist power? Berg himself accurately captures this tension as "between radical critique and moderate recommendations", which is damning in its accurate depiction of the obvious stalemate which encompasses any claim to radicalism within the imperial mainstream to say the least.

Intellectual Radicalism after 1989 is a sobering scholarly testament to Berg's clear-sighted devotion to the primacy of empirical research, as he compiles an impressive array of theoretical wreckage and geopolitical failure as aspirations towards a socialism, which by its sheer historical emphasis on materialist causality, never actually materializes in history. And yet, simultaneously implicit in the work itself is an unremitting persistence of Marxist critique as an emancipatory imperative of redemption within modernity itself as a concerted systematic opposition to the contemporary behemoth of globalized capital.

However, was it not Sartre, who warned us explicitly, that "you cannot, with impunity, form generations of men by imbuing them with successful, but false, ideas. What will happen if materialism stifles the revolutionary design to death one day?"[34] If we are to follow the epistemological implications of

---

it rested entirely upon it." Michel Foucault, *The Order of Things*, (New York: Vintage Books, 1966, 1994) p.261.

[34] Jean-Paul Sartre, "Materialism and Revolution", *Literary and Philosophical Essays*, (New York: Collier Books, 1946, 1962) p.256.

Berg's work, indeed, it would seem that such a day is now upon us.

Reveries of the Ronin

green tea, cigars & existential liberation – As the outsider, overlooked, and held in suspicious contempt, if not pragmatic disregard, I work in undisturbed solitude amidst the boisterous noise and postmodern social gravity of New York City's eroding literary café culture. As a radical intellectual, implicated by an insistent wager on the creative tension of spiritual autonomy situated against established structures of power, my thought interrogates the Real and enunciates Revolt by confronting structural injustice through an insurgent philosophical commitment that seduces insight through critique.

I write continuously, compulsively, as passersby bear witness to a sullen dialectic mediation between human agency, a ballpoint pen, a couple of notebooks, a cigar and a laptop computer. Sporadic sipping of green tea comprises the only source of interruption, as the ebb and flow of my thoughts engage in rigorous dialogue with contemporaries and forbears towards insurgent contributions to the philosophical reasoning and Black liberation discourse of these times in which we live.

On occasion, I spontaneously break an irrepressible rhythm of intellectual endeavor by purposefully stepping outside the café entrance. Being there, I stand out, alone though not aloof, and begin lighting my cigar. Afterwards, intermittent cigar puffs renew a creative transcendence imbuing Honduran tobacco smoke with a certain reflexive texture as it travels up and about, rising above the fray.

Amidst our comings and goings as everyday people, it doesn't take much, be it a furtive head nod of acknowledgement, or briefly locking eyes out of curiosity, to recognize the oneness of humanity directly implicated by an *intersubjective resonance* of mutual recognition that existentially precedes the essential scope of our common praxis, as interactions moving about searchingly towards the world and tellingly towards one another.

Surrounded by a landscape of behemothian materiality that threatens to eclipse all perspective, I gaze skyward towards a horizon that allows me to trace ever rising wisps of cigar smoke with phenomenological appreciation of unrestricted movement and unfiltered ascendancy as generated by intentionality, stainless steel lighter and pure tobacco. A few more puffs, and I return inside the café and steadily resume my intellectual endeavor, thus actualizing my lived temporality implicated by the decision to write as an incredibly singular mode of engagement in the world and lived rhythm of praxis that constitutes my human subjectivity.

And yet, the sound of a police siren nearby intervenes, foreshadowing the structural-inert violence that mediates against the lived immediacy and fleeting temporality that situates my capacity within the contingent force of historical circumstance to constitute 'being-in-the-world' as Black subjectivity. Writing implicates my existence in the face of the normative gaze of modernity as an assertion of Black subjectivity-as-human 'being', and thus interrogates potentialities of radical ontological freedom with an urgency disclosing horizons of emancipatory praxis that must of necessity sustain the irreducibility of human agency and its irreconcilability with the Real.

Arising from human 'being' structurally positioned as the *underground of modernity,* the exceptional antagonism of Black subjectivity exists as *defiance* to the normative gaze, distinguished by *dread* as a mood of movement from inauthenticity towards social persecution, rather than an existence of *anxiety* within the normative gaze, indicative of *anguish* as a mood of motion from self-deception towards authenticity that characterizes existence structurally positioned in the *imperial mainstream-as-civil society.*

Indeed, the normative gaze of modernity, as imposed by a western imperialist continuum, threatens the ascendant humanity of Black community with *biopolitical pacification.* Thus, the universal scope of insurgent philosophical endeavor is situated precisely by the irrevocable human singularity of lived Black experience.

café culture, intellectual engagement and the Ronin – As a singular and demanding mode of engagement in the world, writing involves the zealous cultivation of a solitude which all too often encourages either simulative hyperactivity or pious inaction in the face of an insurmountable mortality that situates the human condition. Indeed, struggle for survival, social priorities, economic considerations, pursuit of leisure, media overindulgence, fetishization of technology and the monotony of daily routine, are all potent concerns with which to preoccupy the implicated temporality of our existence against the possibility of embarking upon the sea of such solitude through intellectual endeavor.

Is it any wonder then that between the creative world of intellectual endeavor and the bewildered herd of rational animality there endures such a formidable abyss of lived experience? And in what sense is this contrast in existential disposition of human 'being' towards solitude, explicitly rendered problematic by the enigmatic figure of *the Ronin-as-radical autonomous intellectual* engaged in literary praxis while encompassed by the condensed plentitude of *intersubjective resonance* at a café? No doubt, writers can be notoriously temperamental and fickle about where and when to write, and what works for one writer can be a definitive roadblock for another.

To be sure, because of the lived duress generated by the lower economic yield that often accompanies autonomous intellectual endeavor, consistent sightings of such writers at work at a café shouldn't be as rare as it is.

And yet, when it comes to seeing some literary action, you are much more likely to find students working on papers or professors busy preparing lecture notes than a creative intellectual engaged in writing. Does this mean that unless you are a student, professor or somehow chained to another type of literary utilitarian motive to write, that you have no 'business' writing? The Ronin writes from a spiritual autonomy of intellectual engagement that exists in constant jeopardy of lapsing into pragmatic, academic or activist registers of thought. However, what is it about the autonomous trajectory of intellectual undertaking that not only characterizes the Ronin, but also allows for such a rewarding and tumultuous love affair between writer and café culture to flourish?

The Ronin writes against imperial mainstream currents of professionalization and activism that often succeed in threatening autonomous intellectual engagement with social extinction. Sartre relates the story of a young imbecile who once wrote that in order to be an engaged intellectual you should join the Communist Party.[35] Now the ideological descendants of that same imbecile claim that in order to be an engaged intellectual you have to first become an academic, contribute your expertise as a commodity to liberal or conservative wings of the ruling power elite for consumption during the news cycle, and then take

---

[35] Jean-Paul Sartre, *What is Literature? and Other Essays*, (Cambridge: Harvard University Press, 1948, 1988) p.23.

advantage of social media platforms to shore up your following. Indeed, as Edward Said makes quite clear, "the cult of expertise has never ruled the world of discourse as much as it now does in the United States, where the policy intellectual can feel that he or she surveys the entire world. . . . even though the United States is actually full of intellectuals hard at work filling the airwaves, print and cyberspace with their effusions, the public realm is so taken up with questions of policy and government, as well as with considerations of power and authority, that even the idea of an intellectual who is driven neither by a passion for office nor by the ambition to get the ear of someone in power is difficult to sustain for more than a second or two. Profit and celebrity are powerful stimulants."[36]

As such, there is no need to regard that oft hurled epithet of being a 'café intellectual' or *café philosophe* as even the least bit insulting. Rather, is it not a worthy commendation befitting of those who choose to cultivate intellectual endeavor at the margins of time-honored institutions of established power and sanctioned bastions of imperial legitimation?

For the Ronin is no officially credentialed expert at the beck and call of established power, wielding stone tablets of certification with the heavy hands of a pundit while in search of neatly packaged solutions to pre-heated problems towards preserving the good conscience of the imperial mainstream. Nor does the Ronin write within a preapproved discursive trajectory

---

[36] Edward W. Said, *Humanism and Democratic Criticism*, (New York: Columbia University Press, 2004) p.123.

adhering to a fixed respectable discipline while amassing institutional legitimacy, social acclaim and prestigious awards towards careerist advancement.

However, to regard the Ronin as a one-dimensional activist cathartically enamored with *protest-as-ritual event* who begrudgingly writes to somehow force feed loud and instantly comprehensible pedestrian prose to the heedless masses out of sheer pragmatic need to organize political agitation, is also a grave mischaracterization. "That means clearly that we are writing against everybody, that we have readers but no public."[37] No doubt, the Ronin writes against imperial consensus and its discontents with an aesthetic edge of emancipatory relevance and intellectual rigor that swords discerning readers from sedated public. For whereas both academics and activists serve vitally important social functions within the imperial mainstream-as-civil society, the Ronin's decision to write 'unprofessionally' discloses a spiritual autonomy of literary undertaking that situates potentialities of intellectual endeavor beyond utilitarian considerations.

Indeed, "one does not write to earn one's living."[38] Now, this Sartrean injunction against whoring out your Muse, does not suggest one cannot "earn one's living" by writing, or even by teaching. Rather, it speaks to that creative intentionality which distinguishes intellectual endeavor from its reducibility to

---

[37] Sartre, p.214.
[38] Sartre, p.164.

professional or activist pursuits, though it can and often does encompass both.

And yet, what is it about the café that ultimately attracts swarthy outsiders, epistemologically disconsolate rebels and metaphysical heretics of the normative gaze? If it is true as West asserts, that "the contemporary Black intellectual faces a grim predicament. Caught between an insolent American society and an insouciant Black community, the African American who takes seriously the life of the mind inhabits an isolated and insulated world."[39] Then perhaps, by providing a constantly changing and varied plenum of social proximity to an intersubjective resonance of everyday people, might café culture somehow mediate against the severity of isolation that afflicts the lived trajectory of intellectual endeavor? One has but to recall that even Malatesta, unimpeachable in the anarchist orientation of his rebellion against established power, never apologized for indulging in café culture towards furthering his radical undertakings, even while literally on the run from police.[40]

Still, there is nothing inherently meaningful about the lived correlation between the Ronin and the urban archipelago of cafés that situate such discip-

---

[39] Cornel West, "The Dilemma of the Black Intellectual", included in bell hooks and Cornel West, *Breaking Bread: Insurgent Black Intellectual Life*, (Boston: South End Press, 1991) p.131.
[40] Enricco Malatesta, *At the Café: Conversations on Anarchism*, (London: Freedom Press, 1922, 2005).

lined cultivation of literary praxis. However, it is this very meaninglessness which is the condition of possibility for the Ronin to impose actual meaning through literary praxis upon the café itself as a contested territory for creative undertaking and intellectual endeavor.

Indeed, is it not this exacting ambiguity of meaning that often discourages writers from taking advantage of the café? Inundated with distractions of Spectacle and hyperproliferation of information, how does the contemporary writer resist the temptation of ceding too much time and agenda-setting legitimacy to the pedestrian punditry of social media? Although obviously a protean apparatus of imperial surveillance contributing towards a totalitarian security culture, no one can dispute the naked communicative efficiency of social media towards expanding the scope and heightening the urgency of intellectual endeavor, even while it necessarily discourages the enigmatic rigor of philosophical thought to appease the instant epistemic gratification of the bewildered herd.

As such, writers in this contemporary era necessarily encounter difficulty finding creative refuge within the condensed plentitude of intersubjective resonance that informs café culture and ultimately challenges the careful cultivation of that solitude which accompanies literary praxis.

And yet, it is in overcoming prohibitive obstacles to thought that inscribes intellectual endeavor with an indelible aesthetic vigor of spiritual autonomy and creative intentionality. Indeed, overreliance on the external trappings of idyllic serenity meant to entice and pamper insight introduces a distinct constellation of limitations towards potentially demeaning the radical imagination itself.

It is rare, of course, to find any writer, including the Ronin, arguing against the clear effectiveness of cultivating solitude in the privacy of a study, retreat or office space. Though not every intellectual has such resources at their disposal, and for this reason the café becomes an invaluable advantage.

However, it is even rarer for a writer to embrace the egalitarian potentialities of creative duress associated with café culture and still resist ceding the emancipatory relevance of intellectual rigor to a condescending accessibility of thought which claims to reach the masses by mirroring forth an abiding spiritual deference to authorized structures of meaning. Wright reminds us that "these tasks are imperative in light of the fact that we live in a time when the majority of the most basic assumptions of life can no longer be taken for granted. Tradition is no longer a guide. The world has grown huge and cold. Surely this is the moment to ask questions, to theorize, to speculate, to wonder out of what materials can a human world be built."[41]

Indeed, harmonious acclimation to the normative gaze gives vent to a mediocrity of thought by loyal retainers of the status quo who preserve the good

---

[41] Richard Wright, "Blueprint for Negro Writing", included in *Richard Wright Reader* edited by Ellen Wright and Michel Fabre, (New York: Da Capo Press, 1937, 1997) p.49.

conscience of the imperial mainstream-as-civil society within a therapeutic literature of average situations by refusing to interrogate the conditions of its possibility. The attractiveness and 'common sense' reasonability of writing like everyone else, especially when you are trying to reach as broad an audience as possible, is extremely difficult to overcome. Such rationality produces riveting displays of discursive conformity as the essential experience of intellectual freedom. "It is when he is acting like everyone else that he feels most reasonable . . . it is in displaying his conformism that he feels freest."[42] As such, by assisting in naturalizing the social coherence of imperial topography, the purveyors of this therapeutic literature of average situations fundamentally veil the lived coloniality that distinguishes the *underground of modernity* from the *imperial mainstream-as-civil society.*

And yet, the condensed plentitude of intersubjective resonance within the café allows for less shelter from the *intermediative gaze* of one another towards one another, regardless of one's lived positionality to established structures of power.

For what is a café, if not a canopy towards sheltering all manner of human subjectivity by the very possibility of dialogue and conversation, no matter how banal, poignant, critical, elevated or contentious? And is not the Ronin, by interrogating the Real and enunciating Revolt through literary praxis, involved in an intensive dialogue within a lived circumference of

---

[42] Sartre, *Literary and Philosophical Essays*, (New York: Collier Books, 1945, 1962) p.108.

philosophical contemporaries, discursive predecessors, potential readers and hostile public?

No doubt, for even by doing no more than effectively serving coffee and tea in a timely, pragmatic and utilitarian manner, housed within an atmosphere that encourages the *intersubjective resonance* of an intermediative gaze, the café enables a qualitative spontaneity of informal dialogue and intentionality of unabridged reflection as lived potentialities of intellectual endeavor accessible to everyday people, and thus infinitely suitable to the intellectually engaged temperament of the Ronin.

allegory of the Ronin – The epistemological clergy of Empire are legion, smugly basking in their cozy relation to a western imperialist continuum that orders the world according to the dictates of capital and racist dehumanization, colluding through materialist orientation towards an ever more perfect globalization of permanent *coloniality in the Raw*. These imperial retainers, loyal samurai of the status quo, function as gatekeepers of public discourse presiding over an unprecedented global cultural hegemony that encompasses both the Academy and the Streets with sanctioned structures of meaning.

And yet, even as these obedient watchdogs continue to hone the normative gaze and polish the prestige of Empire, a writer enters the fray with swords drawn against the authoritative source of their discursive legitimacy. Who is this disheveled outsider, this swarthy literary rebel of ill repute, this fearless iconoclastic thinker from the underground of modernity who dares challenge the epistemic sentinels of established power through the sheer potency of insurgent philosophical discourse?

Rugged, uncouth and intemperate, *the Ronin-as-radical autonomous intellectual* introduces epistemic ruptures against the normative gaze towards destabilizing the conditions of possibility that forcibly maintain and globally consolidate Empire. Engaged in continuous discursive onslaught against established structures of meaning, the Ronin remains resolute in maintaining an emancipatory dialogue with both the

Academy and the Streets without leaning too heavily on either for ultimate legitimation.

The Ronin and the imperial samurai exchange fierce gazes of tempered mutual contempt across a bridge, not unlike the *Sirat*[43], without a trace of either ceding any sign of recognition between them, thus spiritually indulging a mounting antagonistic reciprocity of epistemic alterity. The normative gaze of modernity constitutes the Ronin as a seditious upstart, uncredentialed rogue thinker and dangerous usurper of discursive authority. The emancipatory gaze of the Ronin *sees* the multitude of imperial clerisy marshaled against him as well-trained watchdogs, professional bootlickers and discursive lackeys of established power. No quarter is asked; none is given.

Emboldened by the prestige of imperial sanction and the pragmatic lure of financial gain, combined with the sheer facticity of their numerical advantage, these obedient retainers of Empire find themselves regularly squaring off in cultured literary opposition to the growing insurgent philosophical encroachment of the Ronin. Yet with each intellectual melee, these loyal samurai fail to properly cope with the pyrrhic

---

[43] Arabic word literally meaning – Bridge. In reference to Islamic messianic tradition, the Sirat is a bridge that is as sharp as a razor and as fine as a strand of hair that the sincere will have to cross on Judgment Day to be counted among the righteous. My own theological reading of Bahai Faith suggests Judgment Day as a day like any other, and therefore, the Sirat can be understood as symbolic of the immense challenges and severe trials which characterize the spiritual path each human 'being' must face as lived potentialities of existential movement towards the Divine.

conditions of epistemic possibility that compel them forward to meet the Ronin's challenge on an existential premise that threatens the discursive authoritarian framework of scientific rationality that shapes their *weltanschauung*.

For the Ronin thrives in the Raw of insurgent philosophical commitment, towards interrogations of the Real and enunciations of Revolt that call into question the epistemic veil of objectivity that protects established structures of meaning with a discursive legitimacy divorced from the lived gravity of sociohistorical consequence. A veil of objectivity that therefore flourishes in stale positivist deference to the Real as constituted by the normative gaze of a western imperialist continuum.

Thus, the Ronin writes as emancipatory praxis that commits thought towards a discursive confrontation with established power by introducing epistemic ruptures against the normative gaze of modernity.

Emancipatory Epilogue

global pandemic, Black liberation & the plague of Empire – We did not choose this global pandemic. Nor did we choose a western imperialist continuum that plagues lived Black experience with an incessant monotony of structural-inert violence against human 'being'. No matter, they are both ours now.

Indeed, regardless of whether the origin of this global pandemic turns out to be benign, nefarious or even tragically accidental, we are now responsible for it. However, such existential responsibility does not equate to being in control of a situation, but rather equates to being able to exercise human agency up until and against the very limits of our mortality within any given situation. This dynamic of radical ontological freedom mediated by the disastrous contingency of history thus contributes towards the possibility of giving meaning to the world in all its irrevocable immediacy.

Our existential responsibility of constitutive self-determination that confronts this world of contingency with potentialities towards the imposition of purpose, is purely indicative of the fact that there can be no ontological divorce between human agency and the force of socio-historical circumstance that mediates against it. As such, any deterministic escape into materialist causality, idealist dogma or linguistic sophistry is rendered trivial by this vital metaphysical tension that implicates the human condition with a lived temporality.

Human 'being' can thus be characterized by the irreducibility of our agency and its irreconcilability with the Real – that exhaustive necessity and tangible materiality of nature, culture and history against which consciousness is temporally situated. As such, the dialectic intermediation of call and response between human 'being' and the Real, is not only the very course of radical ontological freedom, but also an existential reservoir of emancipatory imperative towards socio-historical Revolt.

No doubt, even before the onset of this global pandemic, an ongoing plague of Empire readily discloses the absolute contingency of existence and the comprehensive ambiguity of meaning that situates the assertion of Black subjectivity-as-human 'being' as an exceptional antagonism within modernity bearing the ontological burden of socio-historical struggles for human liberation against western imperialist power. As such, lived Black experience finds itself as standard bearer of universality for the human condition itself.

To be clear, although the Truth of universality informs our human singularity as lived Black experience, Truth is not tradition or culture; it is not a given in history, but rather intervenes against the sedimentation of history, tradition and culture by rupturing the normative gaze and breaching the Real through emancipatory praxis.

This global pandemic, in facilitating conditions of possibility for a world encompassing break from the normative gaze, can assist in potentially disrupting previous unreflective modes of 'being-in-the-world' embraced by dominated non-resisting masses from too easy a reification back into conventional routine, arbitrary pursuit of leisure and daily grind of survival.

And yet, how might we avoid being led blindly back into convincing reconfigurations of coloniality that reinvest geohistorical legitimacy and accompanying economic resources into a violent topography of imperial coherence that structurally sustains the oppression of ascendant humanity as a socio-ontological underground of modernity dehumanized through 'race', exploited through class and juridically criminalized as foils to an imperial mainstream-as-civil society that sees itself as at least nominally 'white', if not typically hyperbourgeois, and in an eager global cosmopolitan accommodationist relation to Empire?

Is there anything we can do to assist one another against a nostalgic return to previous consumerist hallmarks of socio-cultural mediocrity that merely preserve the status quo of advanced neo-liberal capitalist globalization, totalitarian security culture and burgeoning neo-fascist political orientations? Is it at all tenable to pursue this unprecedented rupture of the normative gaze to its limits, whereupon either new potentialities of emancipatory praxis or reactionary blowback surely await?

Contrary to such welcome contributions to political thought by comrades who seek to scientifically eliminate the risk of emancipatory praxis by distilling social change into controllable variables of materialist causality, the streets of history offer no guarantee of outcome. And yet, it is in the streets of history where any wager of emancipatory praxis must be ultimately settled, and there is no way to alleviate the pressing socio-ontological gravity of the decision to Revolt in the face of established power without engagement in struggle.

To be clear, it is precisely because so much about this global pandemic is uncertain and indefinite, with no potential cure in sight or end approaching fast enough, that each measure of our actions in response bristles with spiritual undertones of social commitment. But social commitment to what? An unapologetic return to social stability of the imperial mainstream-as-civil society predicated upon neo-colonial police occupation of Black community, mass incarceration and murderous repression of any assertion of Black subjectivity-as-human 'being' with impunity?

A routine complaint is registered by neo-colonial police about cigarettes being purchased with a supposedly counterfeit twenty-dollar bill. And yet, within minutes of arrival on the scene, an officer first draws his gun then holsters it while barking at George Floyd to put his hands on the steering wheel of his vehicle.[44]

---

[44] Narrative of events leading up to the murder of George Floyd and all ensuing transcribed quotations based on "How George Floyd was Killed in Police Custody", Evan Hill, Ainara Tiefenthaler, Christiaan Triebert, Drew Jordan, Haley Willis and Robin Stein, nytimes,com, May 31, 2020.
https://www.nytimes.com/2020/05/31/us/george-floyd-investigation.html

Ninety seconds of dialogue between them gives way to neo-colonial police combatively dragging Floyd out of the vehicle. These same police agents abruptly place handcuffs on Floyd and then sit him down on the sidewalk with his back against the wall of a nearby restaurant. After sitting peacefully for six minutes, neo-colonial police coerce Floyd closer to their vehicle and begin forcing him inside. Now stumbling to the ground under the weight of increasing police violence, Floyd alerts them for the first time to the fact that he is having trouble breathing as they contentiously grapple with and then shove him inside their police car.

Soon another vehicle of occupying imperial power arrives, which makes it a total of four neo-colonial police who now gang up and turbulently force Floyd back out of the police car and then subdue Floyd, who is already in handcuffs, face down on the concrete.

As one neo-colonial police agent looks on and runs interference against anybody gathering nearby who might dare provide Floyd with any assistance, another policeman stubbornly secures Floyd's legs while yet another applies undue pressure to Floyd's torso. The fourth neo-colonial police agent acts accordingly and succumbs to a banality of structural-inert violence against human 'being' by routinely lodging the brunt of his knee against Floyd's neck in flagrant methodical disregard for humanity itself.

Floyd himself continues voicing alarm at the predicament of his very humanity while still literally face down on the street. Even with the increasing weight of three neo-colonial police bearing down upon him and his mortality, Floyd somehow finds the human agency to communicate a phrase he will repeat at least sixteen times within the next five minutes –

"I can't breathe."

A telling attempt at dialogue ensues between a neo-colonial police agent charged with violently imposing the sovereign legitimacy of established power upon Black community, and George Floyd structurally positioned as ascendant humanity giving voice to the universality of lived Black experience as human 'being' against Empire.

"I can't breathe man, please."

One of the neo-colonial police agents responds by pretending to be incredulous to the situation –

"What do you want?"

Floyd then employs facts in an attempt to pragmatically reason with the oppressor –

"I can't breathe, please, a knee on my neck. I can't breathe sh*t."

A nearby friend begins to panic and resorts to yelling clear and adamant instructions at Floyd, all the while hoping that the neo-colonial police will somehow follow suit and allow his exhortations to be realized –

"Well get up and get in the car man!"

George Floyd responds to his friend in a way that attempts to simultaneously convince an imperialist occupying force that he intends to cooperate –

"I will."

The powerless friend frustratedly tries again–

"Get up get in the car!"

Floyd then reminds his friend, while hope-fully also reminding a neo-colonial police agent who has yet to even flinch, much less remove his knee from Floyd's very neck, that –

"I can't move".

And yet, the eventual murder of George Floyd for merely asserting Black subjectivity-as-human 'being' does *move* us to resistance by reawakening tremors of an exceptional antagonism that can erupt at any given moment towards *insurrection-in-itself* being decided in the streets of Empire.

"I've been right with the whole thing."

By bringing himself to account, Floyd discloses dread as lived Black experience confronting the brutal ambiguity that there is no ethically right action or wrong action before the normative gaze of western imperialist power that alleviates the relentless targeting and biopolitical pacification of the human condition itself through unremitting neo-colonial police violence against Black subjectivity.

Indeed, the objective violence meted out by neo-colonial police force is not contingent upon the ethical behavior, legal, moral or social, of the oppressed. For such violence is structural-inert, an active originary violence reconfigured as passive structural relations of power over generations and generations by sheer monotony of systematic renewal and institutional sanction. The *normative gaze* of western imperialist power is reliant upon such *objective vio-*

lence in tandem with *miseducation of soul* towards necessitating a lived *coloniality*, often framed as 'racial' or sometimes class and even nationalist based distinctions, between an *imperial mainstream* as people who merit human consideration, and a *socio-ontological underground* as populations who are deemed unworthy of ethical human regard. Objective violence thus assists in constituting the sovereign legitimacy of Empire upon precisely such gratuitous measures of oppression meant as biopolitical pacification against any assertion of human subjectivity amongst the oppressed.

"Mama."

As the shadow of death encroaches upon his very existence, George Floyd enunciates a poignant Yearning of spirit, for the Woman whose very labor and love ushered him forth into the world, against the rapidly unfolding inevitability of his own murder at the hands of four neo-colonial police agents.

Floyd's friend still refuses to cease in his exhortations–

"Get up and get in the car right!"

After eight minutes and forty-six seconds of neo-colonial police marauders violently compressing his legs, back and neck into the concrete–

"I can't. I cannot breathe."

"Look at him" – a bystander implores to no avail. For in refusing to look at George Floyd and *see* in him an affirmation of our shared humanity, neo-colonial police everywhere must now deal with having to *look at him* in the whirlwind of *insurrection-in-*

itself. Indeed, and in looking at him we *see* a binding universality of the human condition rekindled in the lucid flames of Black Rage as Molotov cocktails fly against hypermilitarized police repression of freedom and dissent. Police vehicles that run over and through protesters[45] end up overturned or set on fire, and at the epicenter where the murder of George Floyd took place, an entire neo-colonial police precinct burns to the ground as insurrection-in-itself spreads throughout the streets of Empire.[46]

Whenever impending death is no longer socially experienced as an exotic abstraction existing somewhere else that only affects the Other 'race', as a rational signification of sub-human 'objecthood', meriting no human consideration whatsoever according to the normative gaze of modernity, it can imbue potentialities of life with meaning at its most urgent. No doubt, who could have foretold that protest-as-resistance and spontaneous rebellion would be the answer to how we decide to spend our time, now that social filters of spectacle, entertainment and distraction, along with technological engines of cultural hyperstimulation are suffering a loss of prestige in the face of this global pandemic that brings the uneventful

---

[45] https://www.cnn.com/videos/us/2020/06/29/detroit-police-drive-into-protesters-mh-orig.cnn,
https://www.theguardian.com/us-news/video/2020/may/31/new-york-police-cars-filmed-driving-at-george-floyd-protesters-video

[46] "George Floyd: Protesters Set Minneapolis Police Station Ablaze, bbc.com, May 29, 2020,
https://www.bbc.com/news/world-us-canada-52844192

prospect of random death to our doorstep at its most neo-liberal?

The tense unity of *protest-as-resistance* and *spontaneous rebellion* globally sets in motion a geohistorical dynamic of *insurrection-in-itself* across the streets of Empire as hundreds of thousands of everyday people, students, lumpenproletariat, adults, youth, rebels and activists, rediscover ourselves as ascendant humanity, and by choosing ourselves as ascendant humanity in resistance against the normative gaze of western imperialist power, the universality of the human condition experiences potentialities of renewal through Revolt.[47]

Indeed, the plague of Empire is reliant upon *the normative gaze* for ideological self-justification through objective violence and miseducation of soul towards veiling socio-historical conditions that structurally undermine our shared universality of the human condition.

We may die tomorrow from the global pandemic, or even tonight by the unaccountable and objective violence of neo-colonial police. And yet, the sheer proximity of our mortality is nothing new to lived Black experience. Rather, is it not the fleeting temp-

---

[47] https://www.axios.com/george-floyd-death-sparks-global-protests-photos-790f29a4-588f-4ce1-b66d-e4dc86bfaafd.html, https://www.washingtonpost.com/graphics/world/2020/06/10/how-george-floyds-death-sparked-protests-around-world/, https://www.bbc.com/news/world-us-canada-52969905, https://www.nytimes.com/2020/06/06/world/george-floyd-global-protests.html

orality of existence that compels us to give meaning to our lives and to the world around us? And by choosing Revolt in response to this plague of Empire, we disclose, rediscover and redefine the mortal contours of the human condition itself precisely by struggling in unity as ascendant humanity for Black liberation.

For the human condition is always already an imperiled presence towards self, engagement in the world and intersubjective resonance towards one another, the plague of Empire upon lived Black experience just makes this *lived rhythm of praxis* even more pronounced in all of its universality.

Without question, decisions to engage in a tense unity of protest-as-resistance and spontaneous rebellion, as insurrection-in-itself amidst this global pandemic, build towards greater social commitment against the plague of Empire at a time that assuredly raises the socio-ontological stakes. Due to this geohistorical situation, questions that severely implicate our temporality can no longer be postponed without a fight. And in choosing to resist injustice in defense of the assertion of Black subjectivity-as-human 'being', we recognize that such an exceptional antagonism introduces imperatives towards human liberation that cannot be satisfied within this contemporary world ordered according to the precepts of a western imperialist continuum. To be clear, the socio-historical relevance and ontological implications of Black liberation struggle against Empire disclose racist dehumanization as a fundamental fault line at the core of modernity and introduce new lived potentialities towards redefining the geohistorical scope of universality through emancipatory praxis.

Scholars, researchers and journalists will one day look back upon us and survey these unsettling times we are now living through, with an objective tone of rationality meant to convey the work of a disinterested observer, engaged in discovering an obviously and empirically sensible narrative. A narrative that is methodically supported by the scientific analysis of facts, figures and events that will ultimately go a long way towards judging contemporary social movements based upon future historical outcomes thus rendering our era of insurrection-in-itself both comprehensible *and* reasonable to the normative gaze.

And yet, the lived temporality of this era is exclusively ours alone to act upon and thus ours alone upon which to impose meaning. Let us not pretend however, to know exactly how this will all end up, and let us fully embrace the Truth that we do not have to know. We struggle for social justice, not because we are prophets, but because we are principled. It is not some unknown future which will eventually explain to us the meaning of what we are doing. We have but to live this very struggle for it to bestow meaning upon us right now.

As a consequence, even as it eludes us in the media coverage of our actions as the normative gaze attempts to make us see ourselves from the perspective of established power, we are still responsible for granting meaning to the struggle through our various modes of engagement, through our diverse ways of 'being-in-the-world', through our social commitments, and through the lived rhythm of our collective praxis.

For as neo-colonial police run rampant, beating us down and assaulting us in the streets for attempting to hold them accountable through protest-as-resistance for the accumulated slaughter of Black people, it is we who will decide in that very moment of radical contingency whether to manifest our unrivaled love for humanity by appealing to the good conscience of the oppressor or through fighting back by any means necessary against the oppressor. And it is in the lived struggle emerging from a combination of both that generates historical movement towards fundamental social change.

No doubt, we know for certain that plenty of mistakes can and will be made in any authentic struggle for Black liberation. Even more so however, we know for damn sure, that the only mistake we can't ever afford to make is to spiritually abandon any grassroots struggle for Black liberation or water down its exceptional antagonistic singularity. To be clear, it is precisely and only when Black lives matter that all lives finally matter. The radical universality of Black liberation struggle has never been more geohistorically imperative than today, which is why this contemporary wave of *insurrection-in-itself* is definitively all about brothers and sisters like Ahmaud Arberry, Breonna Taylor, Adama Traore, Giovanni Lopez and George Floyd.

For this struggle is about a world encompassing imperative towards an authentic egalitarian universality of the human condition in confrontation against western imperialist power. And yet, in as much as this latest uprising of Black liberation is accurately recognized as being worldwide in scope, such Black liberation movements speak to a growing consciousness that is so much more than global. We can feel it tangibly as an *intersubjective resonance* of unity-as-diversity during each wave of protest-as-resistance and spontaneous rebellion. For in challenging the normative gaze of Empire with socio-historical exigencies of Black liberation that ultimately cannot be met within the established structures of globalized order, a trajectory of emancipatory praxis that is almost *geonational* in scope becomes manifest.

As such, whenever geonational *insurrection-in-itself* engulfs the streets of western imperialist metropoles in the name of Black liberation, as protestors, activists and lumpenproletariat risk their lives in vigorous street confrontations and clashes with neo-colonial police and their self-deputized collaborationist allies, we can never forget that such resistance involves a constitutive ontological risk and demanding socio-historical wager over whether it will be the oppressor or the oppressed who has the last word upon the universality of the human condition.

Working Concepts, Discursive Terms & Unfixed Definitions

Alienation – process or condition of estrangement from the radical ontological freedom that characterizes human 'being'. Not to be confused with the more severe condition of dehumanization. Confronting alienation can lead to a lived experience of anguish. See **anguish, dehumanization**.

Alterity – condition of otherness as the refusal of recognition or relation of separation as the absence of reciprocity.

Anguish – lived apprehension of human 'being' as irreducible agency that is irreconcilable with the Real of any given situation. Anguish arises from the recognition that there is no substantive 'empirical self' that predetermines our actions or natural essence that justifies our behavior. Rather, there is a radical ontological freedom experienced as a kinetic distance of interiority or 'presence-towards-self' that makes us not only responsible for our actions, but also responsible for the possibility of bringing meaning to the world through our actions. Whereas dread is associated with dehumanization and the underground of modernity, anguish is associated with alienation and the imperial mainstream. See **alienation, dread, imperial mainstream**.

Anthropology – refers not to the academic discipline that bears its name, but to an underlying theoretical framework and guiding discursive conception of what it means to be human.

Anti-slavery dialectic – open ended dialectic movement of the Revolt of human 'being' against *chattel* slavery as call and response to the disaster of history.

Ascendant humanity – communities of everyday people awakening to the emancipatory universality of their particular socio-historical struggle for liberation.

Bewildered Herd – dominated non-resisting masses behaving in impotent obedience to the normative gaze of established power.

Biopolitical – rooted in *chattel slavery*, the overdetermination of lived experience through the regulation of bodies towards social control of populations.

Biopolitical danger – resistance designated by the normative gaze as so corrosive to the imperial mainstream-as-civil society that it calls into question the sovereign legitimacy of western imperialist power and thereby threatens the socio-historical stability and imperial topographical coherence of modernity. See **exceptional antagonism, normative gaze**.

Biopolitical pacification – exercise of power through mechanisms of coercion accompanied by objective violence towards promoting the abdication of human agency by materialist reduction of the human condition through comprehensive regulation and/or deregulation of populations as bodies according to logics of 'race', occurring so structurally consistent that overt racism becomes an unnecessary blemish to the prestige of established power.

Black liberation discourse – insurgent orientation of emancipatory thought as initiated by the anti-slavery dialectic of Revolt against western imperialist power.

Black radical thought – insurgent orientation of emancipatory thought that fundamentally calls into question the racial anthropology, sanctioned epistemology and sovereign legitimacy of a western imperialist continuum.

Black Rage – unheralded lucidity of Revolt. Piercing clarity of affective indignance as consciousness venturing towards voicing an incommunicable reckoning of emancipatory praxis.

the Blues metaphysic – speaks to the possibility of a radical beginning as a vast reservoir of emancipatory creativity, imagination, aesthetics and discourse initiated through call and response of lived Black experience to the disaster of history as a constant improvisational search for provisional foundations of upheaval from which to approach questions of the human condition, freedom, liberation, Justice, universality and the Divine without recourse to equilibrium, guarantee of stability or necessity of resolution, completion or wholeness.

Civil society – exists within the imperial mainstream between public and private spheres as a terrain of rights, liberties, political consent, common interests, social influence and collective pursuits where hegemony is contested and produced while implicitly dependent on the ongoing socio-ontological stability of established power. See **imperial mainstream**.

Coercive anonymity – structurally consistent disregard of human 'being' imposed by the normative gaze of established power towards rendering particular populations 'invisible' to human consideration, ethical treatment or legal redress.

Coloniality – deterritorialized positionality of racist dehumanization as violent structural-inert relations of power inscribed within modernity itself that sustain and define lived hierarchal intermediations between imperial mainstream and socio-ontological underground of modernity.

Dehumanization – process or condition of reducing human 'being' to 'objecthood' as a materialist determinism that negates, interrupts and suppresses potentialities of human agency, with the aim of establishing the foundation for a generalized withdrawal of human consideration, ethical treatment and legal redress by the normative gaze of established power. Not to be confused with the less severe condition of alienation. Confronting dehumanization can lead to a lived experience of dread. See **dread**, **alienation**.

the disaster – enslavement and racist dehumanization of human 'being' as the socio-ontological basis for modernity.

the Divine – absolute transcendence of the Real as unforeseen opening, sublime possibility and/ or inexhaustible horizon of meaning.

Dread – lived apprehension of the human condition as irreducible agency that is irreconcilable with the Real of any given situation in the face of inevitable socio-historical persecution. What distinguishes dread from anguish is lived positionality to established power. Whereas anguish is associated with alienation and the imperial mainstream, dread is associated with dehumanization and the underground of modernity. See **dehumanization, anguish, underground of modernity.**

Emancipatory praxis – constitutive self-conscious struggle and socially decisive engagement that unifies thought and action towards potentialities of human liberation.

Empire – deterritorialized sovereign legitimacy of ongoing asymmetrical reconfigurations of western imperialist power structures that are inscribed with racist dehumanization and coloniality towards globally consolidating the interests of concentrated capital as manifest in totalitarian security culture, indefinite expansion of military forces on the international front and hypermilitarization of police forces on the domestic front. See **western imperialist continuum, western imperialist power.**

Empirical self – reduction of human 'being' to materialist determinism as the substantive basis of a fixed identity. See **human 'being'**.

Exceptional Antagonism – speaks to the conditions of possibility for a decisive fundamental challenge to established power that breaks through the normative gaze by radically disrupting the sovereign legitimacy of a western imperialist continuum and thus cannot be reconciled within the prescriptive boundaries of modernity. A perpetual socio-ontological imperative towards the emancipatory possibility and universality of Revolt.

Existential liberation critique – insurgent philosophical orientation that reveals a radical questioning of the human condition, in correspondence with socio-historical struggles of human liberation, that builds upon original interrogations of the emancipatory thought of Frederick Douglass, Jean-Paul Sartre and Frantz Fanon.

Geonational – contemporary horizon of emancipatory praxis that introduces geohistorical potentialities of egalitarian social structures sustaining world community towards overcoming advanced neo-liberal capitalist globalization by transcending nation-state boundaries of an asymmetrical world ordered by a western imperialist continuum.

Hegemony – domination to the point of achieving popular legitimacy whereby even the oppressed participate through the commodification of consensus in perpetuating their own ongoing subjugation. See **civil society, imperial mainstream, normative gaze.**

Human 'being' – temporally embodied consciousness situated in the world against the Real through a kinetic distance of interiority that introduces radical ontological freedom as irreducible agency that is not only irreconcilable with the Real, but in constant lived intermediation against culture and history. Thus, affirmation of human 'being' realizes itself as renunciation of 'objecthood' and all attempted formulations of materialist determinism. Human 'being' is the basis of human subjectivity, but not its equivalent thereof, as human subjectivity is constituted through constantly achieving and renewing praxis without resolution towards developing a temporal and distinctive rhythm of 'being-in-the-world'. See **kinetic distance of interiority, human subjectivity.**

Human subjectivity – self-defining intentionality that arises from human 'being' as resistance against the Real and lived intermediation with temporality, culture and history. Human subjectivity is constituted and continuously reconstituted through lived rhythm of praxis as simultaneous presence towards self, engagement in the world and intersubjective resonance towards one another. See **lived rhythm of praxis.**

Identity – locates and secures a substantive 'empirical self' through stable positionality to the Real and harmonious relation to the normative gaze of established power. Identity mediates against the irreducibility of human agency and as such, is a furtive achievement of human 'being', not the equivalent of human subjectivity, though it shares the same basis. See **empirical self, human 'being', human subjectivity**.

Ideology – epistemic closure and cultural reification of a particular system of thought as absolute. Ideology is generated by the normative gaze of established power. See **normative gaze**.

Imperial mainstream – globally designated cosmopolitan populations that merit human consideration, ethical treatment and legal redress according to the normative gaze of Empire based on race, class or nationality. See **civil society**.

Imperial topography – superimposed asymmetrical positionality of the imperial mainstream over the socio-ontological underground of modernity as a rational coherence and hierarchal arrangement of historical features and cultural consolidations of western imperialist power. Implicitly represents the natural order of the world according to the normative gaze. See **positionality**.

Insurgent philosophy – emancipatory thought that interrogates the Real and enunciates Revolt against the normative gaze from the underground of modernity at the crossroads of Truth, meaning and power.

Insurrection-in-itself – lived dynamic unity of protest-as-resistance and spontaneous rebellion as unregulated social movement towards reopening history to the conditions of possibility for human liberation.

Intersubjective resonance – mutually heightened reciprocity in the Raw disclosed as the immediacy of lived experience between one human 'being' and another that reverberates with constitutive significance and social potentialities towards human subjectivity and community by evoking the prospect of adversity as a catalyst of movement towards unity or towards conflict.

Kinetic distance of interiority – threefold dynamic of situated consciousness as constitutive self-determination (consciousness introduces meaning to the world), relentless transcendence (consciousness surpasses the situated present) and spiritual upheaval (consciousness uproots the constituted past) that discloses the human condition as a continuous 'presence-towards-self' rather than an 'empirical self'. see **human 'being'**.

Lived rhythm of praxis – self defining intentionality and temporal movement towards the world and intersubjective resonance towards one another as the trajectory of human 'being' that constitutes human subjectivity. see **human subjectivity**. see **praxis**.

Lived universal – dynamic unity and universal relevance achieved through singularity of lived experience situated in the disaster of history.

Miseducation of soul – epistemological indoctrination and ideological coercion towards abdicating the irreducible agency of human 'being' in favor of objecthood, rational animality or a fixed 'empirical self' as modes of materialist determinism. Miseducation of soul works in tandem with objective violence towards constituting the normative gaze. See **normative gaze, ideology**.

Modernity – post-traditional social structures accompanying the contemporary nation-state as historically imposed through an ongoing praxis of imperial conquest, genocide, colonial expansion, industrial revolution and human slavery, while ideologically proclaiming belief in evolutionary social progress, scientific rationality, democracy, technological advancement, human rights, mass production, standardization, division of labor, urbanization and economic development. Although modernity is often associated with the decline of religiosity, it would be more accurate to suggest that modernity merely introduces Race, Nation and Capital as a new pantheon of gods that now easily compete with and often eclipse the Cause of God in terms of authentic religious devotion.

Neo-colonial policing – counterinsurgent use of domestic police force as an occupying army to manage local populations and subjugate nascent potentialities of Revolt through hypermilitarization, civic initiatives and zero tolerance measures towards preserving socio-ontological boundaries between the imperial mainstream and the underground of modernity.

Normative gaze – unreflective imposition of established power upon situated consciousness that overdetermines-from-without through objective violence and miseducation of soul. The normative gaze preempts both the enunciation of spontaneous thought in ordinary discourse and the articulation of formal rationality in academia, as an epistemological self-justification and ideological frame of reference towards constituting the topographical coherence of the Real in legitimating concordance to the imperatives of established power.

Objecthood – ultimate aim or condition of dehumanization that reduces human 'being' to a materialist determinism that negates, interrupts and suppresses potentialities of human agency, so as to establish a foundation for maintaining a generalized withdrawal of human consideration, ethical treatment and legal redress from the normative gaze of established power. See **dehumanization**.

Objective violence – structural-inert violence that is both sanctioned by and reproduces the sovereign legitimacy of established power towards achieving such a repetitive degree of systemic frequency that it rationally escapes social notice and historical scrutiny out of sheer familiarity. Objective violence works in tandem with miseducation of soul towards constituting the normative gaze. See **normative gaze, structural-inert**.

Ontology – questions fundamental structures of being, existence and reality. Focuses on '*what* there really is' rather than '*that* there actually is'.

Overdetermination-from-without – coercive interventions towards supplanting human subjectivity by imposing 'objecthood' upon human 'being' as a fixed identity based on constant external reinforcement by the normative gaze of established power. See **normative gaze, identity**.

Phenomenology – questions the direct immediacy of reality with a descriptive philosophical emphasis on how the world is experienced as it initially appears to consciousness. Focuses on '*that* there actually is' rather than '*what* there really is'.

Positionality – lived hierarchal correlation of human 'being' to the topographical coherence of established power as constituted by the normative gaze, often the basis of identity. See **Identity, imperial topography.**

Postmodern lumpenproletariat – emancipatory unity of race, class and international outcasts arising from both imperial mainstream and socio-ontological underground of modernity against Empire towards introducing the possibility of geonational egalitarian community.

Praxis – self-conscious struggle and socially decisive engagement that unifies thought and action towards both constituting the Real and introducing meaning into the world. Consistent praxis develops a temporal rhythm that often serves as the initial basis for constituting human subjectivity out of the radical ontological freedom of human 'being'. Praxis can also refer to systematic action organized by established power towards constituting the Real. See **lived rhythm of praxis.** See **human subjectivity.**

Presence-towards-self – kinetic distance of interiority that characterizes the human condition as temporally situated consciousness in tandem with engagement in the world and intersubjective resonance towards one another. See **kinetic distance of interiority.**

Protest-as-resistance – collective action that disturbs the sovereign legitimacy of the normative gaze by an ascendant humanity that confronts established power with an emancipatory gaze of Revolt. Social praxis of collective unity as movement towards questioning and disrupting the boundaries of civil society in the name of Justice.

Protest-as-ritual event – reduction of protest to liberal-democratic passion plays that function more as catharsis for the imperial mainstream rather than as effective resistance to established power. Characterized by an unwillingness to question the boundaries of civil society in the name of law and order.

Race – rational signification of subhumanity epistemologically masquerading as a neutral scientific category to classify the intrinsic diversity of humanity and stabilize it into a fixed order of hierarchal identity according to the normative gaze of Empire.

Rational animality – subordination of the irreducible agency of human 'being' to biological determinism.

the Raw – metaphysics of lived intensity and almost binding proximity.

the Real – non-conscious plenitude and exhaustive materiality of existence that is drenched in culture and history and thus both situates the human condition and mediates against it.

Reciprocity – mutual recognition, dependence, action or influence.

the Ronin – allegorical designation of independent radical intellectual engagement.

Revolt – phenomenon that introduces ontological significance to socio-historical rebellion.

Socio-ontological – refers to binding questions of socio-historical relevance and ontological consequence, thus ultimately calling into question the very structure of reality. See **Ontology**.

Structural-inert – structural embodiment of praxis as passively comprehensible.

Underground of modernity – the wretched of the earth. Race, class and international outcasts condemned by a western imperialist continuum to suffer through coloniality as a perpetually underdeveloped, underprivileged, undereducated, underrepresented, underclass of modernity and who therefore merit no human consideration, ethical treatment or legal redress under the normative gaze of established power.

Western imperialist continuum – socio-historical continuity of a comprehensively administered power structure of racist dehumanization and coloniality in all its varied manifestations and consistent reconfigurations spanning from European invasions of the Americas, beginning in 1492 on through today in our contemporary world of advanced neo-liberal capitalist globalization. See **Empire**.

Western imperialist power – socio-historical imposition of a heavily administered power structure of racist dehumanization and coloniality permeated by imperatives of domination and exploitation through concentrated capital, indefinite expansion of military forces on the international front and hypermilitarization of police on the home front. See **Empire**.

Wretched of the earth – the socio-ontological underground of modernity. Race, class and international outcasts. See **underground of modernity**.

* * * * * * * *

www.ingramcontent.com/pod-product-compliance
Lightning Source LLC
Chambersburg PA
CBHW020257030426
42336CB00010B/800